19

# THE
# TEXAS
# BREED

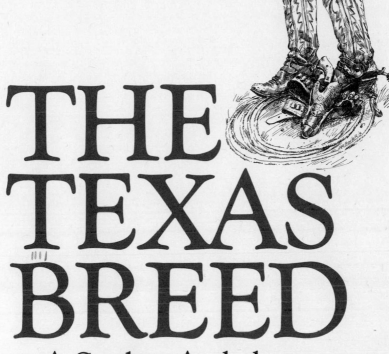

# THE TEXAS BREED

## A Cowboy Anthology

by DON HEDGPETH

### NORTHLAND PRESS · FLAGSTAFF

*Line drawings by Joe Beeler.*

*To my dad, V. W. Hedgpeth,*
*and my grandfather, O. D. Smith*

# CONTENTS

# ILLUSTRATIONS

*O. D. Smith, Bandera, Texas, cowboy, 1915* (author's collection)

# INTRODUCTION

"THE COWBOY originated in Texas." With this short sentence, J. Frank Dobie summed up simply, completely and accurately the initial chapters in anyone's history of the North American range cattle industry.

The cowboy is the proudest figure in the rich and vital heritage of the Lone Star State. The foundations of Texas are tied hard and fast to cattle and to the men who work around them. A verse which almost all young Texans used to learn in school proudly proclaims:

> Other states were carved or born,
> Texas grew from hide and horn.

The influence of the cowboy on Texas is both dramatic and indelible. It provides a flavor that is an essential part of Lone Star heritage. This same influence figured prominently in the history of the entire Trans-Mississippi West, where longhorn cattle and Texas cowboys were the vanguards of civilization.

One of the original "ring-tailed tooters" of the open range, Teddy Blue, remarked upon the impact of the men from Texas: ". . . the Texas cowboy's mode of speech and dress and actions set the style for all the range country, and his influence is not dead yet."

An article in one of the rarest of all range cattle books, *Prose and Poetry of the Livestock Industry of the United States,* published in 1905, observes:

Among the old-time cowboys the Texans and those of Texas antecedents were the most efficient for all-around work on the range and on the trail. Nearly all of them lived and moved as if they had been born in the saddle and had seldom been out of it since. They hesitated about doing anything outdoors on foot, and if they had to go but a few yards they would mount their horse for the journey—a habit, however, that was but little less fixed among the entire fraternity. While all cowboys had to be good horsemen, the Texan was, it would seem, as skillful and daring a rider as he could have been were he and his pony grown together.

Joseph G. McCoy founded Abilene, Kansas, and promoted it as the first substantial market for Texas trail herds in the period following the Civil War. His opinions of Texas cowboys were not complimentary. In his book, *Historic Sketches of the Cattle Trade of the West and Southwest,* published in 1874, McCoy wrote:

The life . . . is one of considerable daily danger and excitement. It is hard and full of exposure, but is wild and free, and the young man who has long been a cowboy has but little taste for any other occupation. He lives hard, works hard, has but few comforts and fewer necessities. He has but little, if any, taste for reading. He enjoys a coarse practical joke or a smutty story; loves danger but abhors labor of the common kind; never tires of riding, never wants to walk, no matter how short the distance he desires to go. He would rather fight with pistols than pray; loves tobacco, liquor and women better than any other trinity. His life borders nearly upon that of an Indian . . . wherein abounds much vulgarity and animal propensity. . . . the most rude and primitive modes of life seem to be satisfactory to the cowboy.

A more fanciful and entertaining picture of the Texas cowboy was offered by Alex Sweet and Armoy Knox in the 1883 book, *On a Mexican Mustang through Texas*. The authors state:

The cowboy is a man attached to a gigantic pair of spurs. He inhabits the prairies of Texas, and is successfully raised as far north as the thirtieth degree of latitude. He is in season all the year round, and is generally found on the back of a small mustang pony, wild and savage as a colt of the Ukraine. This fact has given rise to a widely diffused belief that the cowboy cannot walk, and he is often cited as an instance—a stupendous manifestation, in fact—of the wonderful working of nature to adapt her creatures to the circumstances surrounding them. It is argued that once the cowboy was a human being—a biped with the ordinary powers of locomotion—but that during the course of ages, becoming more and more attached to his horse, and have gradually ceased to use his legs, these important adjuncts have been incapacitated for pedestrian uses, and thus the cowboy and his pony have developed into a hybrid union of man and horse—an inferior kind of centaur.

Some scientists, however, dispute this, as several specimens of the cowboy have been seen, from time to time, who, wandering into the busy haunts of man, have—under the influence of excitement, and while suffering from intense thirst—been seen to detach themselves from their mustangs, and disappear into business houses, where their wants were attended to by a man wearing a diamond breast pin and white apron.

But it is again that great Texas writer and collector of cowboy books, J. Frank Dobie, who has best classified and defined the Texas cowboy. He delineates him as ". . . an evolvement from, and a blend of, the riding, shooting, frontier-formed southerner, the Mexican-Indian horseback worker with livestock (the vaquero), and the Spanish open-range rancher. . . . The driving of millions of cattle and horses from Texas to stock the whole plains area of North America . . . enabled the Texas cowboy to set his impress upon the whole ranching industry."

I grew up in a part of Texas where the cowboy tradition still runs deep. When I was a young boy there were plenty of Mexican and Anglo punchers in the South Texas brush country, and there still are. Small towns like Alice, Kingsville, Banquete, Agua Dulce and others sprung up originally to serve the needs of the outlying ranches. Genuine, double-tough brushpoppers can still be seen on their streets. These men made the historical figure of the cowboy much more real to me than the heroes of the Alamo, or the movie-star cowboys of Saturday matinees ever were.

I'll always remember the old brushpopper who hired on with a watermelon harvest I was with one summer when I was fifteen. This greying, bowlegged puncher had never done, or known, anything but cow work. He was an Anglo, but had spent so many years back in the brush that he had forgotten most of his English and was at ease only in speaking Spanish. He never took the spurs off his boots the whole time he was with us.

One of the men spent almost an entire morning showing the old cowboy how to shift the gears on a tractor, and then sent him several miles out of the little town of Realitos to bring in a trailer full of watermelons. It was way past supper time when he got back. The trip which should have taken one

*V. W. Hedgpeth, Texas cowboy and father of the author* (author's collection)

hour took over four. He had driven the tractor all the way out, and all the way back in low gear.

He could not abide the criticism that came, nor the promise of further instruction in the operation of farm machinery. He loaded his "war bag," rolled his bed, and with his big-rowled spurs clanking his agitation, he made tracks back to Hebbronville to hunt a man's job in a mesquite-country cow camp.

I grew up around men like this. The impressions they made on me have endured and are much more vivid than anything I have been exposed to since.

I am proud of the time I was able to spend with the vaqueros in the dense, thorny thickets of Nueces County and other areas of South Texas. I have good horseback memories, too, of the Del Rio country, where the brush was not so thick and the horses were superior. Later, when I spent time on ranches in Montana and Wyoming, I always felt that I had been to a better school.

The harsh economic realities of cowboy life dissuaded me from my boyhood ambition to spend my life in a brasada cow camp. Men who have done so end up with little more to show for it than their memories, aching joints and a thorn-torn hide. But I have not denied my admiration for the breed. I am still preoccupied with the figure, both historical and contemporary, of the Texas cowboy.

This preoccupation manifests itself primarily in my collecting and reading books that deal with range cattle history in general, and Texas cowboys in particular. Next to my wife, Sug, and our boys, Cody and Clint, my "cowbooks" are the things nearest my heart. Sug will, on occasion, question the order of these priorities. This usually happens when I have just bought an old, musty-smelling cowboy book when the boys needed new clothes for school. Most women cannot understand the compulsions of a bibliophile. Sug comes a lot closer than anyone I have known.

The twelve selections I have chosen for this book come from particular favorites in my own library. They present, I believe, a comprehensive insight into the various angles from which we may look at the historical figure of the Texas cowboy. There are many books which are rarer and much better written than the ones I have picked. But I believe these twelve selections, which are autobiographical in the main, will afford the Texas cowboy the opportunity to speak for himself. Heaven knows there have been enough authors, professors, and Hollywood directors who have presumed to interpret him for us. These interpretations, in most cases, would have scarcely been understood, much less endorsed, by the men which they were supposed to represent.

With this in mind, I won't try to offer any penetrating discourse on the subject of Texas cowboys. Instead, may I introduce you to twelve men whose stories are characteristic and true to the Lone Star breed.

# CHAPTER I

# LEE MOORE

LEE MOORE'S STORY is an excellent example of the richness which is often found in many of the more obscure titles in the field of the range cattle history. It appeared in a little fifty-five page pamphlet which was printed in Cheyenne, about 1923, under the title, *Letters from Old Friends and Members of the Wyoming Stockgrowers Association*. The publication of the pamphlet came as a result of a resolution adopted at the 1914 convention of the association to: ". . . gather data for a history of the Association and development of the cattle business in the State of Wyoming. . . ." Only twelve "old friends and members" responded to committee member Harry Crain's request for recollections. The twelve responses, including Lee Moore's were printed in letter form along with a one-page foreward, which ends with the traditional toast of the association: "The Cowman—God Bless Him!"

The story Lee Moore told in his letter to Mr. Crain represents, in a few short pages, a complete story of the Texas cowboy. It would, in fact, be impossible to find a more representative narrative. Moore experienced all there was of the golden era of the open range; from the South Texas cow hunts of the

From *Letters from Old Friends and Members,* published by the Wyoming Stock Growers Association, 1923. Reprinted with permission of the Wyoming Stock Growers Association.

1860s, to driving beef herds in the 1870s, to stocking the ranges of northern grass in the 1880s, to becoming a cowman himself in the 1890s.

In addition to Moore's firsthand participation in the pageant of range history during the era of free grass, the narrative is further enhanced by the humor and zest which characterized the spirit of Texas cowboys in general, and Lee Moore in particular. The flavor and the vitality of the period is abundant in Moore's writing; they form essential elements which are rarely found in the hundreds of books which continue to be written on the subject by men who are more often historians than cowboys.

*Letters from Old Friends and Members* is one of the real gems in any collection of range cattle history books. It was printed for the membership of the association (a relatively small number) and is extremely difficult to find today. Material such as Lee Moore's story makes it a highly desirable item and one which should be eagerly sought by any serious range history collector.

———————

IN 1861, when my uncle, Jack Elliott, started to the War of the Rebellion or to Mexico he gave me an old cow and a little calf, and my father gave me a pony and a bridle, and a sheepskin for a saddle. My cowboy uniform consisted of a straw hat and a long hickory shirt, so at five years of age I was a cattle owner fully equipped for the business, but that winter the old cow died or went to war. As I thought in those days everything went to war but women, children and negroes, and as my little calf was not a heifer, and owing to my age, my herd did not increase during the war, but when the cruel war was over and my father came home, I owned a work steer. My father, knowing my fondness for little calves, gave me a little calf for my steer, and he continued to give me a little calf every spring for my yearling until I was about sixteen. Then I went out of the cattle business by giving the little calf to my sister. In 1866, my father added to my uniform a saddle, overalls, a wool hat, a pair of shoes and started me out reping. Reping in 1886 in Texas was quite different from reping in Wyoming in 1915. We didn't call it roundup in those days. We called it cow-hunts and every man on this cow-hunt was a cattle owner just home from the war and went out to see what they had left and to brand up what I had neglected to brand during the war. I was the only boy on this cow-hunt, and as my little calf was at home with its mother, I was looking for cattle that belonged to my father before the war. We had no wagon. Every man carried his grub in a wallet on behind his saddle and his bed under the saddle. I. P. Olive was boss and I will state here that he was some boss. I was put on herd and kept on herd when we had one and I don't think there was ever a day on this hunt when we didn't have a herd, and I carried a lot of extra wallets on behind my saddle and a string of tin cups on a hobble around my pony's neck. A wallet is a sack with both ends sewed up with the mouth of the sack in the middle. I just mention this for fear some of the cow men don't know what a wallet is. Whenever the boss couldn't hear those cups jingling, he would come around and wake me up. We would corral the cattle every night at some one of the owner's homes and stand guard around the corral. I didn't stand any guard but I carried brush and cornstalks and anything I could get to make a light for those who were not on guard to play poker by. They played for unbranded cattle, yearlings at fifty cents a head and the top price for any class was $5.00 a head, so if anyone run out of cattle and had a little money, he could get back into the game. For $10.00, say, he could get a stack of yearlings. My compensation for light was twenty-five cents per night or as long as the game lasted. Every few days they would divide up and brand and each man take his cattle home, as we now call it— throw-back.

This cow-hunt continued nearly all summer, so in the winter of '66 I started to school. I went to school two or three days nearly every month when there was any school. When I wasn't going to school I was picking cotton or cow-hunting until '69. Father sold his cattle to J. F. E. and F. N. Stiles, and threw me in with the cattle, with the understanding that he would receive $12.00 per month for my services, so you see I began to slip back, owner to rep, rep to common waddie. I worked for Stiles as waddie, top-hand and boss until the spring of 1876, when Stiles sold their cattle and me with them to D. H. and J. W. Snyder. Snyder built some corrals and a branding chute on Turkey Creek on Stiles' range and put their brother, Tom Snyder, in charge of said corral and that was our headquarters. We had no tents, tarpaulins, cabins or anything of that kind. We had a wagon with a cover over it and a little grub in the bottom of the wagon box, which we kept dry. By the way, I had no bed, but used J. W. Snyder's, and when he visited us, he had the pleasure of his own bed with me in it. It was the best bed on the job, consisting of a buffalo robe, one suggan, one blanket and a feather pillow. Snyder hired a big crew of men and started me out with a two-horse wagon, a bunch of saddle horses and some cow boys just from Tennessee and a few Germans from Round Rock to gather these cattle and turn them over to Tom Snyder and to hold and road brand, so I started out as boss of the first wagon I ever saw on a cow-hunt. I had no check book, one reason, I couldn't write a check, and another, there wasn't a man in Texas could read a check, so checks were not in use. Our first stop out from headquarters was for noon. My Kaiser cook came to me, said he had no pan to mix his bread in, so I told him to mix it in the water bucket or top of the flour sack. After dinner I went to feed the work team in the feed box attached to the hind end of the wagon box. I discovered he had mixed the bread in it. After using language to him that would not look well in this report, I put him on a horse and sent him back to headquarters, told him to tell Mr. Snyder to send me another cook and a breadpan, so I put one of the cowboys at driving the team and pulled out for the next camp. The new cook and pan arrived O.K. in time for supper.

I want to speak of our grub as it was my first starting in at high-living. We had flour, coffee, sugar, beans, bacon and some dried ap-

*Young cowboy ahorseback* (National Cowboy Hall of Fame)

ples in a barrel that some northern Yankee had slipped in to Texas to kill off what few Confederates were left in Texas. The cook started in to prepare some of those apples for dinner. He filled a skillet full of them, put in some water and put the lid on, and the first thing he knew, the apples had thrown the lid off and were all over the fire, in fact, they were all over the camp. I don't think any barrel would have held what was once in that skillet, so I ordered them thrown out and prohibited the boys from eating any of them until they got back and found out from Mr. Snyder what they were, but the barrel was handy for the boys to throw their extra saddle blankets in. When we got back and found out they were not poison, we ate nothing but dried apples and drank water as long as the apples lasted, but never had any more cooked.

On this cow-hunt, I saw for the first time a cow boy put sugar in his coffee. We soon got the herd put up. Snyder had all the cows and calves cut out, and turned on the range, and I was put at Olive's ranch to work with them and look after Snyder's cattle. Tom Snyder drove the herd on north, and J. W. Snyder went to buying beef steers of Olive, Sauls, Littin & Tinnin. He would receive the cattle at Olive's ranch, put me in charge of them to drive them to Rockdale, the nearest railroad point, to ship them north, and, as I have said, checks were not in use—the parties selling the cattle would go along and help drive them and get their cash, generally in silver, put it in a sack and take it home. As I boarded with Olive, and as I mentioned the high-living with Snyder, I will mention Olive. They furnished coffee, corn meal, salt, whiskey and beef, provided you didn't kill one of theirs. We would sometimes get out of coffee or meal or salt but never out of whiskey or beef. Some unknown parties, not in favor of Olive's way of doing business, on the night of August 2, '76, slipped up and set the ranch on fire and the shooting began. When the smoke cleared away I was running across the prairie with my life and night clothes and a Winchester handed me by a dying Olive. I don't know whether it was loaded or not, but I was afraid to drop it for fear the attacking party would hear it fall. The first time I saw Mr. Snyder after that, I resigned, and picked cotton the balance of '76. January 1,

'77, I rented land and put in a crop. When I got the net proceeds of that crop in my pocket, I started to the Bryant Agriculture Military College to finish my education. The habits I had contracted while a cowboy and persisted in following, did not meet with the approval of the college officials and I finished in fourteen days, so I went back to my old employer, J. W. Snyder, at Round Rock, and hired out to him as common waddie, to go down on the coast and help drive a herd of cattle to old Cheyenne. Tim Hamilton was the boss to Julesburg, Colorado, where Snyder turned over several herds to the Ilif outfit, and I came on to Hillsdale below Cheyenne, with Bob McMurday as boss. Here Snyder delivered cattle to Alex Swan, John Sparks and others, and Mr. Snyder took us all to Cheyenne and paid us all off in Ben Hellman's store, so I presented myself to a new ducking, blanket-lines suit of clothes and sallied forth to see the sights of Cheyenne. McDaniel's Theatre was running full-blast, so there I went; so the next morning I soaked my forty-five colts so as to have a little jingle in my pocket and began looking for a job. I got a job with Tom Branson's outfit, Dave Knight as foreman. John Sparks was interested in the outfit—that is, we had a lot of 4J cattle. We branded the cattle at Ex-Governor Carey's ranch on Little Horse Creek, and then drove them to where Douglas now stands. We camped over night at what now is the State Fair Grounds. The next morning we turned about half the herd across the river. We turned the balance loose on the north side, and the wagon went back to Cheyenne for more cattle. The boss was down with the rheumatism, so he and the cook, Frank Merrill, Bill Ward, Bumpus, one of the partners, and I, were left here to build a ranch. Merrill and Ward cut the logs and hewed them on LaBonte and I hauled them with two yoke of steers. We had just about completed the house, when we got word Branson had bought the Red Bluff ranch, at the mouth of Elkhorn, so we moved down there. He had bought the ranch alright—and trouble with it.

The man he bought the ranch off went to work for him. It seemed the place belonged to W. C. Irvine, who owned the ranch then that Jim Shaw now owns, and was our closest neighbor. Alas! it wasn't long before we got acquainted with Mr. Irvine, for one day as Daily, the man who sold the ranch, the boss, cook and myself, were quietly eating our dinner in Mr. Irvine's cabin, Mr. Irvine poked a Sharps rifle in the door and demanded possession. Mr. Irvine and Daley began to have some warm words and as there was no window in the cabin and that gun was too large for me to pass it in the door, I asked Mr. Irvine to please raise it that I might get out under it. This was my first meeting with our honorable Treasurer, and for many years President of this Association. So he had our stove thrown out and his put in, and when he left and we were sure that he was in Cheyenne, we threw his out and put ours back, finished our house and put in the winter there. But Irvine finally got the ranch. In the spring our wagon started out. I think they worked from Fort Laramie up the north side of the river to Fort Fetterman. We had a small two-horse wagon, two little mules hitched to it; no tents, stove or mess-box, nor any convenience we have these days. Branson and I went with the OU wagon, Joe Hazen, foreman. The roundup started April 1, '79, at Fort Fetterman and worked up the north side of the river to the mouth of Poison Creek. We would swim our cattle across the river every day as we would work the south side later. The wagons never left the river. We drove all the tributaries to the camp on the river and rounded them up. We drove the cattle sometimes thirty or thirty-five miles. When we had worked all the country north of the river that we deemed necessary, we came to Fetterman and crossed the river on the old government ferry boat, then worked up the south side to old Fort Casper. There the first roundup I was ever on in Wyoming broke up. That summer I formed a partnership with Sam McGatlin and we were very successful in poker playing, monte dealing, and horse racing, and we bought twenty-two head of old cows of Branson and he said we could work and run our cattle with him. My partner and I concluded I had better go back to Texas and buy some yearlings, put them in with some herds coming up and come up with them and he would work on for Branson. As he was not known in Texas by the name, I consented to go, so I went to Chicago with a train of cattle. After spending a couple of weeks in Chicago and visiting all the prominent cities of Texas I had never seen, about the time the grass started I wrote my partner that I didn't believe that I would buy any yearlings, but if he wanted any and would send me his money, I would invest it in yearlings and come up with them. He wrote back that he had been in Cheyenne a month, and didn't think he wanted any yearlings; that he had sold our cows for a big profit to a half-breed Indian on credit; that the Indian had resold them for cash and had gone to parts unknown and that he was leaving that day for Idaho. I haven't seen him or the Indian since, but I came up the trail alright in the spring of 1880, with Morris & McCutcheon cattle. The boss quit at Ogalalla and the herd was turned over to me to hold until it sold, which was not long. I then went to work for the O–O outfit, Hanner and McKaulley as owners, Joe Stratton as fore-man. We drove the herd to Antelope Springs and turned them loose. In '81 I was rep on Powder River. That summer I drove beef to the railroad to ship to market, 3,500 head all told. That winter I went to Texas. January 4, '83, I was married in Texas, and in the spring after I came back, I was put in as a foreman of the O–O outfit, at $125.00 per month and a check book.

I could handle the men and the cattle alright, but the check book was considerable trouble. It gave me some notoriety, as I received a great many letters from bankers whose letters were all notifications of overdraft. In '84, I was made foreman of the roundup from the mouth of Black Thunder to Fetterman. This roundup was known as the Lance Creek roundup. A. Spaugh was foreman from beginning somewhere east of Lance Creek. My wages were raised to $150.00 per month. This was the first year the mavericks were ever sold, and the proceeds went to the Association. The foreman was required to give a bond and sell all mavericks every ten days and send the proceeds, with the ten per cent, to Tom Sturgis, who was the Secretary of the Association. My first sale was to Metcalf and Williams. I put M on the neck—the Association brand, and Williams put his brand on them. When I sent in my report, Mr. Sturgis wrote back saying it was not the intention of the law to sell those yearlings to little thieves like Metcalf and Williams. I sold the next bunch to W. P. Ricketts, who wasn't any better in my estimation, than Williams. I continued to run this outfit until the bad winter of '86 put them out of business. So in the spring of '87 I started in to run the O–K and G–M outfit. It had taken me about seven months to find out that they had no cattle, and I told them so.

I began to realize that the cattle were getting scarce, and so were jobs, so I bought a few cattle in '87. In the spring of '88, for the first time in my life, I found myself without a job, so I ran the general roundup from Lance Creek west. In '89 and '90 I worked for the Ogalalla outfit, run a wagon when there was any cow work to do. In '91 I established my first cow ranch on the head of the Belle Fourche.

The laws of Wyoming required a man to brand his calves before they were a year old and as a great many of the cowmen violated that law by not branding their calves, I adopted some of those neglected yearlings and put my brand on them so the cowboys would know whose they were, and also to increase my herd. I followed that industry until '99, when I discovered that the legal talent, so necessary for my business, was so expensive that my profit was not sufficient to carry on the business and eat regularly, so I sold out and left Weston County with some regrets, a lot of good friends and no bad debts, and came to Converse County and bought Royston's Ranch on Lightning Creek, with a few horses and cattle. I didn't have stock enough to make ranching pay, so in 1902 I went into the First National Bank of Douglas, with my breath stronger than my intellect, and after knocking over a couple of clerks and getting by the cashier, I found Mr. J. DeForest Richards, President of the Bank, in his private office, and after making my cross and a lot of promises, I borrowed some money to buy cattle with. I bought some two-year-old southern steers. I run them for two years and shipped them to Omaha and when I had them all shipped out, I found that I had lost the interest and my labor, but consoled myself that I was a cowman and could borrow money, and that I had had the use of those steers for two years, and that I would never buy any more until I could fatten them.

So here I am, in 1915 still borrowing money and buying cattle, and if I ever die, which I think is very doubtful, I will still have that little calf to hand down to my grandson, little Lee Moore.

# CHAPTER II

# FELIPE

THE ORIGINAL TEXAS COWBOY was a Mexican vaquero who was at home in the mesquite jungles of South Texas. It was from these brush-popping vaqueros that the Anglo cowboys originally learned their craft. The adventures of Felipe and the other vaqueros of the Rancho San Juan provide one of the very few insights into this important part of the story of the Texas cowboy.

The book from which this story is taken is classified as fiction; yet it is faithful to the place, the time, the country, and the characters of the old cow outfits below the Nueces River in Texas. The author, John Houghton Allen, came to know, and to understand the country and the men he writes about while living on the Rancho Randado, one of the oldest and most historic of all the ranches in South Texas. Allen's book is singularly distinguished in its treatment of a segment of the story of the cowboy that has been ignored by nearly all of those who have written on range history. Additionally, Allen writes with a polished literary style that is seldom discerned in western fiction, particularly that which deals with the cowboy.

Felipe and the other men who take part in this story were the mold from which the Texas cowboy was cast. The creed of

From *Southwest,* by John Houghton Allen, published by J. B. Lippincott, 1952. Reprinted with permission.

these men who "lived with their ropes tied to their saddle horns and their saddles cinched on broncs" was: "Kill thy horse, kill thyself, but rope and hang on." It was a creed which had its origins in the brush country of South Texas and was carried by Texas cowboys from the Rio Grande all the way to the prairies of Alberta.

I highly recommend *Southwest,* and Allen's little volume, *San Juan* to anyone who is interested in the antecedents of the Texas cowboy. They also represent a literary maturity and accomplishment that is outstanding in range fiction. *Southwest* is still fairly easy to obtain. *San Juan,* which was privately printed in an edition of 420 copies, with illustrations by Harold Bugbee, is much more difficult to come by.

———

"YOU BELIEVE IN A MAN by the spurs he wears," Ernesto asked me, "or the horse he rides? Then I will tell you of Felipe.

"He came riding out of the brush from Zapata way—it was thirty years ago—on a log-headed brute much scarred by the chaparral. He was a rigid little man, gnarled and bowed and wiry, and a cross-eyed mozo rode behind him like an esquire. There was a touch of the manner about Felipe, he might have been some petty hidalgo, and I shall tell you about the idiot Lili, also. Lili wore fresh hide leggin's over cloud-white pantaloons, and the large rowels of his cheap spurs jingled like castanets. He breathed hard, he jerked at his iron curb, or he rested his palms—an elegant gesture—on the huge pommel of his charro saddle.

"Felipe was practically afoot, accompanied by this clown, he didn't look the part, but he was a vaquero, señor. One of the best. His eyes were bloodshot from the dust. He was lean and fierce and pigheaded, the kind that is kept in the rain and under the stars the year round, paid four bits a day to break his bones and kill good horses, and discarded like an old saddle blanket when his service is done. He worked in the brush, in country you can't get a white man into, and men like him rot in thickets sometimes where they fall.

"Felipe was brave as a lobo. He was no more afraid of spoilt horses or somersaults through the brush than frijoles or tortillas—a valiente he was, a man of blood, passionate and faithful and unforgiving. But we laughed at him; he was ridiculous. He had probably never in his life been laughed at in the dark country he came from, but we could not help it—had he earmarked us each time, we would have laughed.

"He was skilled with the lasso, like all charros, but left-handed and awkward as a woman throwing rocks. He could rope wild boar and antelope, give him the horse to do it on, and in the corral he could forefoot anything, anyway. He adopted our own conceit of roping all cattle with the lariat tied fast to the saddle horn. Other vaqueros rope and wrap on, dally it's called, but we in our pride and skill at the San Juan lived with our lassos tied to the horn and our saddles cinched to broncs. It was the honorable thing, you see, it was what gave us a name—it was the San Juan!

"A steer splitting about on the end of your rope, in the heavy branched thickets, the horse snorting and jumping or bucking outright, the vaquero flipping his lasso on this side and that not to become entangled, forking and yanking his goddamn bronc, dodging brush and high cactus, protecting himself and his fractious mount from the charges of the steer or its weight as the rope went taunt— there was no way in all the world to let go or back down from the job in front of you. Felipe liked that, there was salt in it. He liked being yanked about, he liked the shock and the rage. He had more falls than any of us, but he would land in his droll positions or be so shaken with fury that we would laugh. The coraje, señor, he had the coraje.

"He did not deserve all our laughter, nor did he have a fall every day. He was a great one to celebrate in the village and, when he treated, he had friends. I have seen him laugh and slap his thigh and almost swallow the cigarette that seemed always to be stuck to his lower lip—and drink! The man had a hollow leg, drinking as much

half-blinded by it when you jumped them into a sendero. They were the ladinos, some of them nine and ten years old before we ever caught or branded or sold them. And some of them we never caught, they were wild as deer, and we hunted them down with rifles.

"We combed the brush, we went tracking and hounding and halloing after a glimpse of them in the heavy shadows. It was so hot and still that you would sweat up your jacket like a shirt. The infrequent sight of them was like that of prey to a hunter. It was hell-on-leather and we used to run them down or kill our horses in the trying. It would have been a pretty sight indeed to hunt for hours and days, and then draw up at the first barricade of thorn and cactus—we would get hot after one, and believe me, we would get him, one way or another. We went after them in the thickets as fast as our horses could travel, never knowing when we would be swept out of the saddle by mesquite, never caring whether we killed ourselves, the horse or the ladinos.

"Those were hardy horses that we rode. Spanish ponies, tough as we were. From hoof to shoulder they had no hair from crashing through the brush. They had as much fun as we did. They were like human beings a-hunting in the hot breathless shadows. Their hearts would go thump, thump, against your boot as you waited. They would rear and plunge when they heard the animal breaking through in their direction. Then, stumbling and hopping and wading and crashing through cactus and catclaw and mesquite, they ran through solid walls of brush, they took the bit in their teeth after the ladino. They would have liked to catch it and shake it in their teeth like terriers. We used to let them find their own way and hold on and wait for the first bit of daylight in all that shadow. It would not be the deepest brush in the world in those foothills if you could swing a lariat. We rode hard on the tail of a ladino and we were lucky if we could flick out underhand and snare a hind leg. We had to be skillful and quick and sit back for dear life when the beast hit the end of the lariat. Sometimes he broke it as you would a string. When it held there was enough bawling and crashing about to spoil the most hardheaded siesta, and there was a clearing in that spot when the ladino got through with it. We had to snare the brute around one way or another, flip the slack and catch the other hind leg or tangle him, somehow. There weren't any rules. We had to yank him down and be out of the saddle and have him tied before he got his breath. We had some close calls, working the gravel hills. We used to wipe the sweat from our eyes, listen for the distant halloing and be off after another like men hunting stag.

"You would have snarled at us, señor, coming into camp brush-torn, our horses bathed in foam and blood, limping on two and sometimes three legs, windbroke, foundered, because you are a gringo, even if you are a good gringo, and the sentiment of your people is badly balanced. You would have snarled at our cruelty, our triumphant weariness, our heedlessness, our callous cheer, but we were just doing our job, the kind of job that gringos wouldn't do. It was dirty work, heartbreaking work, and we were nonchalant about it as old Esteban making biscuits at the chuck wagon. Besides, those horses were well the very next morning—they got over their soreness and stiffness quicker than we did.

"Can't you see Felipe in that brush and brutality, the wind and the darkness? He didn't look the part, but it was meat for him. His horse breathing hard after a ladino that frothed at the mouth and ran with stringy muscles, the huge horns shaking. His hat in his eyes, his jacket tattered, cursing his saints, with Lili scrambling after him like an urchin left behind. Can't you see Felipe—earnest and foolhardy and funnier than ever—on the crowbait horse, with that idiot Lili dangling behind him? This fallen impatient petty grandee, and we laughed to remember him, but he was killed in October of that year, in the deep monte of the foothills of the Little Mountains.

"The work was almost done by October. We were on the last quick sweep through the hills and out on the plains that slope to the coast, out of the hell of brush and stillness to the cool white villages and the women at home—anxious for the women like mariners from the sea—crackling through the brush like ladinos ourselves, shouting over miles in a day, in haste to be done, the devil himself stampeding our gathered herds in the night. With black night and thunder and lightning at times, but we would catch them up again at a gallop and be on as before, whooping through the foothills and thinking of the good times and tequila in the cantinas and our women at the windows.

"It was not the last thing in the world you could expect. It was not out of the ordinary, even. The pear was stamped down and there was blood on the shrubs. In an opening was Felipe's off-breed of a horse, dumb terror in its eyes, being jerked about by a red bull that was roped to the saddlehorn. He was jerked to his knees whenever he faced the bull, and he was pulled over backwards on the saddle when they ran in opposite directions—but the strong horsehair girths held. The bull would gore him and run as if it were scared out of its wits. The bull was that quick, he could stomp the horse down and in one clear swoop be at the end of the rope and yank the horse up again. Any other time the rope would have snapped like a line.

"The bull was bellowing like one in the area, but he wasn't mad—he was nimble and terrified, and this anchor of a horse defeated him. But what scared him was the body of Felipe between them, sprawling in the air like a last bad effigy of himself. Just out of the saddle, a spur caught in the fork as he had been dragged from the seat, a twist of rope around his neck as he'd fumbled in his slack, his head almost severed from the body hanging, victim of a monstrous tug-of-war was all that was left of Felipe. The man we laughed at, still in character, but we did not laugh—for the rope was tied to the horn, the San Juan's way, twisted so hard from the strain it had cut to the wood, leaving the smell of tattered leather above the gore.

"Lili was there, too—all arms and legs and lariat, beating his dumpy mare around and about, crying like a baby. We didn't rope the bull down, we rode our horses right into the bull and over him, we knocked him down with a broken shoulder, and then we were off our horses kicking him in the snout senselessly."

# CHAPTER III

# JIM COOK

J. FRANK DOBIE wrote about Jim Cook's book: "Nothing better on cow work in the brush country and trail driving in the 70s has appeared." Cook's adventures on a Frio River cow hunt are similar to those of Lee Moore's story in Chapter One. Together these two pieces give a complete and faithful picture of cowboying in Texas prior to the trail-driving era.

Jim Cook was a greenhorn when he first joined the cow outfit of old Ben Slaughter, which was bossed by John Longworth. The thick and thorny brush along the Frio River breaks were his classroom. The Mexican brushpoppers of Slaughter's outfit, men very much like Felipe from Chapter Two, were Cook's teachers. He learned his lessons well and went on to make a good brush hand and a drover on the Chisholm Trail. Later, Cook became a well-known western figure, hunting big game in Wyoming and scouting with the cavalry after Geronimo in New Mexico. Throughout his life he remained a cowman and died in 1942 at his ranch home in Sioux Country, Nebraska.

An interesting fact for range country bibliophiles is that for a time in the 1880s Cook ran the WS Ranch in New Mex-

From *Fifty Years on the Old Frontier, as Cowboy, Hunter, Guide, Scout, and Ranchman,* by James H. Cook. New edition copyright 1957 by the University of Oklahoma Press. Reprinted with permission of University of Oklahoma Press.

ico. When he quit in 1887, William French, author of the rare range book, *Some Recollections of a Western Ranchman,* succeeded him as manager of the WS outfit.

It was in the mesquite thickets of South Texas that the first chapter of the story of the Texas cowboy was written. Cook's recorded experiences on this subject, along with John Young's story, as told in Dobie's *Vaquero of the Brush Country,* and Lee Moore's little piece in *Letters from Old Friends and Members,* make up about all of the firsthand, and worthwhile, treatments of the brief period following the Civil War when wild cow hunts and brush-popping vaqueros were center stage in the developing drama of the Texas cowboy.

---

EARLY IN THE MORNING . . . , Mr. Longworth and his crew, consisting of ten Mexicans and myself, started on a cow hunt. We took our saddle horses with us, together with the bunch of cattle from which we had killed the beef. We used pack mules and ponies for carrying our provisions and cooking utensils. We had no slickers. Our provisions consisted of green-berry coffee, salt side of pork, corn meal, saleratus, salt, and pepper-berry. Our cooking utensils and dishes consisted of a couple of Dutch ovens, a frying pan, a camp kettle or two, and a coffee pot. We had each a tin cup holding about a pint, together with a tin plate and an iron knife and fork. Sugar was not furnished us. Our pack train generally carried a plentiful supply of black navy plug tobacco and some prepared corn husks for cigarette wrappers. Matches were very scarce in that country, and each man carried a flint and steel, together with a piece of punk or prepared cotton tape with which to build fires or "make a smoke."

We went about five miles from the home ranch and camped near an old corral. The corrals in that country were all made about alike.

A trench some three feet deep was dug in the ground. Strong posts about ten feet long were then placed on end, closely together, in these trenches, and the ground tramped firmly about them. They were lashed together about five feet above the ground with long strips of green cowhide. The gateposts were very strong, and so were the bar poles used on them. These bar poles were always lashed to the fence-posts with ropes when the corrals contained any wild stock. Strongly built wings were run out from the gate, in order to aid the riders when penning stock. Often these wings were built two hundred yards or more in length. What time we had left after reaching the corral, we put in repairing it, as well as the wings, and getting it ready to hold the cattle we had brought with us and any we might be able to catch.

The following morning about sunrise we left the corral, taking with us the decoy herd, Longworth leading the way through the thick growth of chaparral and mesquite. After traveling a mile or more he led the herd into a dense clump of brush and motioned us to stop driving it. Then, telling two men to stay with the cattle, he rode off, signaling the other men and myself to follow him. I fell into line behind all the other riders, thinking that the best place to watch the performance. We rode in single file for probably a couple of miles.

Suddenly I heard a crash ahead, and in less than two seconds every rider in advance of me was riding as if the devil were after him. My horse knew the work, and plunged after the riders ahead. I held up for a moment; then the thought struck me that, if I did not keep those ahead of me in sight, I might never get back to camp. I did not know in which direction we had been riding, and one acre of ground looked just like all the rest—everywhere brush, timber, cactus. I gave my horse the reins, trailing the ones ahead by the crashing of limbs and dead brush. I was kept pretty busy dodging the limbs which were enough to knock me from the saddle and warding the smaller limbs and brush from my face with my arm.

I think I rode all over that pony—first on one side, then on the other; then, as he dived under some big live oak limb, almost under his neck. We crossed several prickly pear patches where the clumps grew from two to ten feet high and about as close together as they could stand. My pony would jump over, knock down, or run through any of them. He was a cow-catcher by trade. He certainly made me "pull leather," and I clung to his mane as well in order to keep in close touch with him.

I had a very strong desire for this chase to end. At last it did. I was in at the finish. All at once I came in sight of one of my Mexican co-laborers. His horse was standing still. The man put up his hand for me to stop, and I did so willingly. He pointed into the brush ahead, and I caught a glimpse of some cattle. A few minutes later I heard voices singing a peculiar melody without words. The sounds of these voices indicated that the singers were scattered in the form of a circle about the cattle. In a few moments some of the cattle came toward me, and I recognized a few of them as belonging to the herd which we had brought from our camp. In a few seconds more I saw that we had some wild ones, too. They whirled back when they saw me, only to find a rider wherever they might turn. The decoy cattle were fairly quiet, simply milling around through the thicket, and the wild ones were soon thoroughly mingled with them.

Every man now began to ride very carefully and slowly, riding in circles around and around them, all except myself singing the melody known as the "Texas lullaby." For all I know, I may have tackled that singing trick with wild cattle for the first time right there, for I was about as excited as the wild cattle were.

After we had ridden around the cattle for an hour or more, I saw Longworth ride out of sight of the herd, dismount, and tighten the cinch on his saddle. He then returned to the herd, and one by one the other riders followed his example. Our horses, having had a badly needed breathing spell, were now in shape for another run. After a few moments Longworth rode away into the chaparral, singing as he went. The Mexicans closed in on the cattle, starting to drive them after him, pointing the herd in the direction of his voice when the brush was too thick for him to be seen. I brought up the rear of the herd. We all kept quite a little distance from the cattle, and each man

*"A vaquero of the brush country"* (author's collection)

tried to make no sudden moves or any sounds that would start a
stampede. At last Longworth led the herd into the wings of the corral, and the wild ones followed the decoys in. The heavy bar poles
were soon lashed.

We had caught some wild cattle, and I had enjoyed a most thrilling experience. My clothing was pretty well torn off; also a goodly
portion of my skin. About nine kinds of thorns were imbedded in
my anatomy. I was ready for camp. We were all hands, as well as our
horses. Such work was a bit hard on both horses and men, but horseflesh was cheap, and men could be hired who enjoyed the work.

The caporal, in leading a string of riders out to circle into the
decoy herd any wild cattle he could find, would not only keep a
sharp outlook for a glimpse of cattle, but he must also be listening for
the breaking of brush or the sound of running hoofs. He would keep
an eye on the ground for fresh tracks of any large bunch of cattle
which he thought he could follow up, until the cattle themselves
could be seen or heard. To go "away around" one of the bunches of
cattle after locating them, and then to circle them into the thicket
containing our decoy herd, meant that the rider must not consider
his future prospects as very bright. It was a case of trusting in Provi-
dence and riding as fast as horseflesh could carry one, regardless of all
obstacles. It was a clear case of "go" from the second the cattle saw,
heard, or smelled a human being.

Not all cow hunts terminated in the manner of my first one.
Many times during my experience hunting cattle by the decoy
method, we not only failed to make a catch, but also lost the decoys.
Some rider, not being able to tell the exact spot where the decoy herd
was located, and becoming confused by the many turns the wild cattle had made him take, would dash suddenly right into the decoys at
the heels of a bunch of fleeing wild cattle. Then, in less than two seconds, there would be a stampede—which simply meant "The devil
takes the hindmost."

The only thing that a rider could do in such conditions was to
single out an animal and, if possible, catch it with his rope. Failing
because of thick timber or bothersome brush, to get his rope on an

animal, he had just one chance left; to spur his horse alongside the fleeing beast, catch it by the tail with his hand, and, taking a turn around the saddlehorn, dash suddenly ahead, causing the steer to turn a somersault. The horse then came to a sudden stop, and the rider jumped off and, with one of the short "tie-ropes" which he always carried tucked under his belt, "bog-tied" the bull, cow or whatever age or sex of cow brute he had thrown. This had to be done quickly, before the animal could recover from the shock of the fall, or trouble would come to the "cow waddie" who had caused it. Flight would not be uppermost in the animal's mind at such a time. The animals did not mind running from a man ten or twenty miles, but when brought to bay by this treatment, their rage would be such that a man would have to take great and sudden care if he valued his life. It would be horns versus pistol should a strong animal regain its feet before its pursuer could tie it down or, failing, be able to get back into his saddle. Tying down wild cattle caught in this manner was a part of the Texas cowboy's trade; and like a lot of other work in this world, it required practice, and plenty of it.

When animals were thus tied down, they were left until we could go to the home pasture and get some more "gentle" ones to be used as decoys. We then drove this bunch of cattle to the place where the wild ones were tied down. If they had been left for several hours, their legs would be so benumbed and stiffened that they could not run fast. The tie-rope was then loosened and the animal allowed to get up among the decoy cattle. Sometimes when regaining their feet they would charge at the nearest live object and keep right on through the bunch of cattle and line of riders. It would then be necessary to rope and throw them again. An animal from the decoys would next be caught and thrown and the two dragged together and tied to each other, by a short rope around their necks, with knots that would not slip. This was called "necking" animals. Sometimes we brought old work oxen from the ranch, to be used for bringing these tied animals to the corral.

Occasionally, when trying to run the wild cattle into our decoy herd, we stampeded bunches of musk hogs or peccaries. When these animals happened to run, crashing and grunting, pellmell into our decoy herd, it often caused a stampede that meant the loss of our decoys, with the exception of such as we were able to rope and tie down.

The captured wild ones gave us plenty of trouble when we started in to train them to be controlled by herders. When we had as large a bunch gathered as we dared to try to hold with only a few herders, we drove them to one of the large pastures owned by Mr. Slaughter and turned them into it. The fences around these pastures were made high and strong, heavy poles being used in their construction.

The day following my first cow hunt, Longworth and the Mexicans went into the corral and cut out part of our decoy cattle. The rest were left with the wild ones. The corral was divided into two or three pens, and these cattle were driven into one of them. They were left there to become used to corrals and also to get hungry, so that, when taken out to graze, they would care as much about food as about regaining their freedom. The first thought of the decoys left with the wild ones, when taken from the corral, was for something to eat and drink. This helped considerably in holding the wild ones with them. Some individual members in each bunch of wild cattle would usually make a dash for liberty the moment they were released from the corral. These would have to be caught and tied down for a while to steady their nerves. Then each of them would be "necked" to a gentle one, to be led for a time. This occurred when we turned our first bunch out.

In helping to control these wild brutes, I was at that time about as useless and helpless an individual as ever graced a cow camp. I could only sit around on my horse and follow along. I did keep my eyes open, and I was there to stay if I could only learn the art of cow-punching. After a few weeks I learned to handle a rope a little, and to do my part in controlling stock that required one to use brain and eye every moment, as well as to be a "range rider." My first few months in Mr. Slaughter's employ made up an experience such as a great many American boys have never enjoyed.

There were other methods used in catching wild cattle, when they became scarce in our immediate vicinity or had become so smart or "up to trap" that a decoy herd would not hold them. One method employed was to hunt them on moonlight nights. This was done in the following manner, when the moon was full:

We would remain in camp during the day, until about sundown. Then we would all ride to the edge of some one of the little bits of prairie about us. Keeping ourselves and our horses hidden in the brush, we would wait for the moon to rise. Then it would not be long before we heard a cow low, a calf bawl, or a bull bellow. It was their feeding time. Sometimes we heard the breaking of brush as they filed out rapidly into the open. Our horses could both see and hear the cattle farther than we riders, and they were trained for this especial work. I think they enjoyed the excitement of the chase. They would seem to know when the cattle were getting close, and at such times they would grow restless and fairly tremble with excitement. All riders, with saddle-girths tightened and ropes in shape for a quick throw, now slipped into their saddles. The moment the caporal thought the cattle were out into the prairie far enough for us to make a quick dash before they could rush back into the dense chaparral, he would give the signal; and, like an arrow from a bow, every rider was off after anything in the shape of a cow brute which he could locate on the prairie.

It was a breakneck game, but good sport for those who liked it. Sometimes a man made a catch with his rope just as an animal dashed into the timber. It was the custom to tie one end of the rope to the saddlehorn. When the rider had the noose end around a big animal's horns, neck, or body, and the animal rushed around one side of a big tree while the rider and horse went on the opposite side, each going at full speed, something had to happen. Either the rope snapped or there was a collision about half the rope-length from the tree. Sometimes a horse was gored to death in these mixups, and a rider had to scramble for dear life.

When pursuing a single animal, it was the custom for a rider to keep up an incessant imitation of a lowing cow. This was done so that, unless too greatly scattered, we could keep in touch with one another. By this means one of us was occasionally able to aid some other rider, in case he had any spare time after tying, or losing, whatever he had started after.

I well remember one little incident connected with these moonlight cow-chasing expeditions. I had tied down the animal I was after and was sitting on my horse—perhaps thinking what a great thing it was to be a cowboy—while I listened hoping to hear someone "lowing" to whom I could be of service. Presently I heard a faint lowing sound that grew louder each moment, indicating that a rider was coming in my direction.

I cleared my rope for action and rode behind a bunch of Spanish bayonet plants close by the trail. I knew that something was ahead of the rider, who was by this time within two hundred yards of me. I soon saw that, if all went well, the beast which was being pursued would pass within a few feet of me. A few seconds later a slick black bull about three years old, dashed past me. I was ready for him, and as he passed I threw my loop over his head. If there was any extra spring in that bull's body, he used it at that moment, with the result that, when he came to the end of the rope, my saddle-girth parted with a loud snap, and I went sailing through space with both feet in the stirrups. My head soon bumped the ground, and by the time the rider had reached me I was needing sympathy or a drink.

I never heard from that bull or that saddle again.

# CHAPTER IV

# JIM McCAULEY

A STOVE-UP COWBOY'S STORY is one of my favorite books from the whole context of Texas cowboy bibliography. It offers a realistic picture of cowpunching that is uncommon among most such reminiscences. Many cowboys who wrote down their recollections in later years tended to regard their experiences from a romantic perspective. This was probably the result of the tone set by the pulp westerns.

Jim McCauley, however, presents his story with all of the harshness and hard knocks that characterized cowboy life. In his later years, McCauley was in bad health and underwent surgery on several occasions—all the result of the tough horses he rode in his younger days. Writing to John Lomax, who arranged to have McCauley's book published, he said: "I wish I had have never saw a cow ranch. Probialy I would not have had to have been cut on and suffered so much. Too many bad horses has been the cause of most of my troubles. While Ide rather be on a cow ranch and work for just wages, be well, have good health, than anything you could name. When you grow up to anything 'tis hard to quit and have to try something else . . ."

The selection from *A Stove-Up Cowboy's Story* offered

From *A Stove-up Cowboy's Story,* by J. E. McCauley, published by the Texas Folklore Society, 1943. Reprinted with permission of the Texas Folklore Society.

here contains nothing remotely resembling the kind of cowboy material to be found in the Zane Grey, or Hollywood interpretations of cowboy life. It is rather the honest, straightforward narrative of a poor farmboy who saw a dignity in cowpunching that cotton picking would never afford him. Jim McCauley's story was repeated hundreds of times as young boys fled their family farms and pridefully accepted the rigors that went along with being a cowboy.

*A Stove-Up Cowboy's Story* is one of four titles published originally by the Texas Folklore Society as the "Range Life Series." The other three books in the series were: *My Rambles,* by Solomon Wright; *A Tenderfoot Kid on Gyp Water,* by Carl Benedict; and *Ed Nichols Rode a Horse,* as told to Ruby Nichols Cutbirth. J. Frank Dobie served as editor of the four-book series. With the exception of the Wright book, I believe the set to be one of the most significant contributions to the written history of the cowboy.

---

O N THE 14TH DAY of August, 1873, I came prancing into this world. I was found in Anderson County, Lone Star State. My first memory was to ride a stick horse and to help hunt for cattle, for every once in a while somebody would go along the big road with a small herd of cattle drifting them west to grass and the prairie country. Then my first wishes and desires was to be a wild and woolly cowboy. 'Twas all I wanted to do but parents went to farming for a living. So I was reared up to be a plowboy instead of a cowboy.

My parents be poor like Job's turkey. They farmed somebody else's land. The other men furnished the land and the team and the plows and a house for us to live in and we then went cahoots in the crop. But to follow a scooter plow in stumps, bare-footed, all day, didn't suit a would-be cowboy.

So my early life was spent on a farm. Things jogged on this way until I was eight years old and my parents started me to school in the little town of Overton. I went by myself—and a country boy in town at school stands a very poor show. They did me every way they wanted to, as Father had told me when any of them done anything to me to go and tell the teacher. But they would lie out of it and I would be the one punished. So I told Father how they done. So he told me the next one that done anything to me to do everything to him but kill him. So next day I was laying for an opportunity to bust them up in business.

At the schoolhouse overhead was a Mason's hall and on this day by some hook or crook they was repairing the house and was building some brick flues and had some scaffolds built up by the side of the house. And at noon I went out of the house to eat my cornbread and sow-belly. Some of them boys had got up on the scaffold, and when I opened my bucket they throwed a half a brick in my bucket. I upped the brick and brought the gentleman off there head first and I kept poking the brick until I had three of them down. A doctor was sent for, and while they was attending the sick, lame and lazy, I skee-daddled for home and told Father. So in his company he went back with me. Father told the professor how I had been treated, how the boys lied on me and I bare the blame, and how he had told me to pestle them up some myself. From that day on I bore the name of Bald Hornet, but I was cock of the walk and crowed when I wanted. It was natural for me, I guess, to be mean.

About this time Father had made a raise some way and bought us a horse and occasionally he'd let me ride it to town or some place in the country. I'd ride with one foot out of the stirrup and sit away over on one side as that was the way I had noticed the cowboys riding. The more I saw of them drifting west, the more determined I was to be a cowboy. Then in 1883 my parents moved west out on the Brazos River in Baylor County. That country was then nothing but ranches, only a nester now and then. It was the home of the cattle kings, as the buffalo had left and the Indians quit raiding on the settlers. Nothing could have suited me more than to be in cow country, as farming didn't set well with me.

In 1888 I was going to a little country school and there was a pretty little miss with blue eyes and golden hair that won the admiration of my heart. I built many air castles with her in them but they all fell through as most air castles do. Another boy quite a lot older and larger than I caused most of my troubles. He undertook to see that I could not talk to her and called me bad names which caused us to fight. In the fight he had me down and was giving me a good, sound thrashing and I was about ready to holler calf rope when his knife fell out of his pocket. When I picked it up he didn't see me, and the blade being loose in the rivet it was not much of a job to open it. I slammed it into him in the hip. I want you to know I did not have to beg him to get off. This girl was one of the first there to see what was wrong. When she saw the blood all over this boy and my hand bloody she thought I had killed him. I told her that she had caused the trouble. The rest of the children went to inform the teacher; so I bid my first love goodby and started for home, which I was not long in reaching.

I told my mother what had happened, and after kissing her a fond farewell I started for the setting sun. I felt that if I stayed there that to prison I would go or that else I would be hung or that boy's father would reck vengeance on me. We lived in Parker County. By nightfall I had walked some twenty miles when I struck a freighter going to Jacksboro. After I had told him what had happened, he said I had done the bully right. After we got to Jacksboro, he kept me at his house some eight or ten days. Next I struck a cow outfit going to the ranch. I struck them for a job and they took me in and in six more days we was at headquarters of the old Figger Eight. They put me to wrangling horses. I thought this was pretty good. It beat being in jail or being hung. The first thing I done when I had worked out money enough was to send and get me a new colt 45 six-shooter, so that if any body come to take me back to Parker County he would

*A proud old cowpuncher* (The Dobie Collection, University of Texas, Austin)

meet with a warm reception. I had blood in my eye and didn't mean to be arrested if it could be helped.

I soon got enough of the horse herding, but that was all they would let me do. But when the fall work was over I stayed at the ranch and cut stove wood and done odd jobs around the place till spring. And when spring did come I had a new saddle and a little pony and some $30 in money. About the first of April I struck north-west as I was determined to go up the trail to Montana. I rode to the XIT headquarters at Channing, Texas, where five trail outfits was fixing to go to Montana. After looking the bosses over, I tackled one called Scanlous John. He looked me over. I was tall enough, but slim was only part of it. He asked me my name and I told him. "Well," he says, "Slim Jim, I don't think you would make a cowboy." I told him if I lived I would, after I hung with him for some two or three days he said, "Well, boy, I'll take you along if you'll promise to go plumb through."

When I got to the XITs, I was broke and I did not have no bed and not much clothes. So poor old Scanlous John took me over to the store and bought me some clothes and a new pair of boots and took me in and let me sleep with him. I'll never forget poor old John for the kindness he showed me when I was a youth and in trouble too.

During the last days of April we got things together to start. He gave me a gentle mount of horses, for which I thanked him with all my heart. On the last day of April we moved out and began to round up to get us a herd. But of all the funny things I had ever saw was the new trail cowboys mounting. Some could ride them and some would ride about two jumps and then there was a horse loose with a sad-dle on. But 'twas fun to me. Beat hoeing cotton or plowing corn. I wanted to try some of those that pitched but I was afraid I could not ride them and as I was doing very well I thought I would let well enough alone.

The first night I stood guard I'll never forget. Standing guard with cattle is like this: The cattle are driven up as close together as they can very well stand and have plenty of room, and are held this way. About dark they will all, or most of them, lay down. And then everybody goes to the wagon, but about two or three. I was put on first guard until 10:30 o'clock. I didn't have any trouble with the cattle, as they lay all right, but I didn't think my guard would ever be out, the time dragged so awful slow. The next morning was a fine day and we was moving on towards Montana, slowly.

On the third night, as usual, I was on the first guard, just Scanlous John and me, and about nine o'clock a black cloud from the northwest come up. I had on my slicker, or oil coat. It began to rain in torrents. The vivid lightning began to flash. The thunder began to roar. And all at once the steers got on their feet an in less time than it takes to tell it they was gone. The night was as dark as ink, only for the lightning. My horse was on his job, so he stayed with the cattle. Every time it would lighten and a loud clap of thunder follow they would change their course, and in a short time I found the herd had split or divided. After some two hours of storm the rain quit and soon it cleared off and the moon shined out, but I didn't know where my pard was or which way the wagon might be.

I had about three hundred head of steers and after everything was still they lay down and I thought I'd see if I could find the other part of the herd. But to my sorrow I could not, so I thought I'd shoot my six-shooter and see if anybody would come or answer me. Bang she went and away went the bunch I was holding. Now I had more trouble than if I had let things alone. After chasing them for an hour, I guess, I got them stopped, but I didn't shoot any more. I saw I was in to it for the night and so I made the best of a bad bargain. Well, the moon in all its beauty came at last and as the sun arose across the eastern horizon in all its glory they never was a poor, wore out sleepier boy than I was.

About ten o'clock a man came in sight. He told me the direction the wagon was. I lit out. I had drifted something like ten miles to the southeast and if any boy ever did enjoy something to eat it was me. If bacon and beans ever tasted good it was then. The boys all told the boss he had lost his tenderfoot, but when they found out I had held a bunch all night they didn't say tenderfoot any more. I thought 'twas the most miserable night I had ever experienced in all my life.

They said it was the way they initiated all the boys, so I took it for granted and hoped 'twould not happen any more.

Things rocked on very well till we struck the Arkansaw River between La Junta and Pueblo, Colorado. It got so stormy up there in the breaks of the Rocky Mountains that we had a storm every night, nearly. Oh, but I did wish I was back in good old Texas plowing corn or hoeing cotton, but alas, I was not, and was made of too good stuff to show the white feather. On we went with a slow but steady gait towards Montana.

My real troubles was yet to come. When we reached the Arkansaw River we went up it three or four days before we crossed. When finely we put into it, it was about level full, as the snow had been melting up in the mountains long enough to swell it until it was a raging torrent. I waited as long as I could before I went in. I didn't get far before my horse got tangled in some drift and sank to rise no more. I had taken off my boots and most of my clothes for fear of something like this. The first thing that come handy was a four year old steer. I got him by the tail and away we went for the other side, which we reached after so long a time. I promised myself I'd never swim the Arkansaw any more.

I had lost my saddle, bridle, blankets and spurs and was broke. What to do I didn't know, but I kept my troubles to myself, and the boys began to guy me about riding bareback until Scanlous John came to my rescue. He told me to ride on the chuckwagon until he could buy me a saddle. He told me the company would pay for me a new outfit. So I felt some better. In the course of a week he sent to Pueblo and got me a new outfit out and out. Then I was one of the boys—a new $45 saddle. But I promised myself that I'd never go up the trail with a herd anymore, that swimming them rivers was just a little bit too dangerous for me.

Finely we came to the last river. It was the worst of them all, and I would not have tried to swim it for all the cattle up there. 'Tis noted for its swiftness and it has two currents. The top current is some two feet deep, and the under current runs twice as fast as the top. 'Twas the noted Yellowstone River. When you got below the top current nothing comes up. 'Tis such a suck to it that to sink in the Yellowstone is a gone fawn skin. When we got there, the other two herds had not crossed. They seemed to be waiting for us. We crossed close to Miles City. It makes the cold chills run over me now to think of that cold water.

One day I went to town just to see what it was like. I had wrote home to mother from way down the country at Pueblo and I told mother to write to Miles City. A letter from her was waiting me. She said the boy I had the trouble with had got well. She begged me to come home. I drawed $50 of my money and sent it to mother. A desire to go back kindly got next to me, but I was determined to go through or know the reason why. So on August 22nd we landed at the headquarter ranch of the XIT in Montana.

After staying a few days taking in the sights, Scanlous John and me prepared to go back to the good old Lone Star State. On the 27th of August it came a light snow and that made me want to get away worse, for any place that it snows in the summer don't suit a Texas cowpuncher, or it didn't me. So I asked John when would we start and how was we going. He told me we would go with a train of beef cattle to Chicago, and from there to Kansas City and then I'd have to buy my own ticket from there on. On the 5th of September we left with a train of beef over the Great Northern Railroad. We fed and watered after they was unloaded at St. Paul, Minnesota. That was the largest city I had ever been in. If I had been by myself I never would have got out of there, but my boss had been a father to me and I done just what he said and everything went all right. 'Twas here that I first saw the great Mississippi River, but I had seen so much water that it didn't charm me much. But the sight of the steamboats—that took my eye. I talked to Scanlous John until he agreed to take a ride on one, so we went up to Minneapolis and back on a steamboat. Next morning we loaded our cattle and on we went to Chicago—the second sized city in the United States.

Nothing would do John but that we must each buy us a suit of new clothes. After visiting the barber shop and having our hair took off some five inches and a good bath—the first I had had since I crossed the Yellowstone River—we proceeded to dike up in new clothes from head to foot. After laying around there two days, I told John I'd have to go on or I'd have no money. We here got our passes reversed to Kansas City and from there I had to buy my ticket. It was here that I had to bid my best friend among cowpunchers good-bye, and from that day to this I have never seen him any more.

After my ticket was paid for and I was on the train I had just $4.60 in my pocket. I left Kansas City in the afternoon and the next afternoon I reached Fort Worth, Texas, just in time to catch a train for Mansfield. Mother was there to meet me. Oh, never was I hugged so much in all my born days and I never was so glad to see anybody as I was Mother. From back some place Mother dug up stuff after we reached home—preserves, jelly, jam, eggs, pies and so on until I began to think I was somebody. We sat up until nearly midnight talking over the past. Mother said I didn't get out of sight until that boy's father and the officer was there to take me in; she said they watched the place for nearly a month before they gave up. After staying around home for a few days father asked me if I didn't think I could pick a little cotton. Well, that didn't sound very good, but nevertheless I began to pick the fleecy staple. I stayed home until spring. I had picked cotton and cut cordwood until I bought me another pony.

CHAPTER V

# "LITTLE BOY"

THE SETTING FOR THE STORY of "Little Boy" and the speckled yearling is West Texas and the historic SMS Ranch of the pioneer Swenson family. The author, Frank Hastings, served for many years as manager of the Swensons' cattle operations and is credited with many innovations in the development of the modern Texas livestock industry.

The story of "Little Boy" is full of the genuine flavor of the Texas cow country. If one could draw a moral from the young cowboy's adventure, it would be that cowboys are made, not born. "Earning your spurs" is a cow-country tradition that is widely honored in Texas. The old-time cowboy song, *Little Joe the Wrangler,* though it ends tragically, deals with the same tradition.

Hastings highlights the quality of cowboy pride in the story of "The Speckled Yearling." Pride was as much a part of the Texas cowboy as his bowed legs and high-heeled boots. This pride was something initially personal, and then extended just as intensely to include the outfit for which the cowboy rode.

Hastings's book, *A Ranchman's Recollections,* was published by a livestock magazine and enjoyed only a limited cir-

From *A Ranchman's Recollections,* by Frank S. Hastings, published by Breeder's Gazette, 1921.

culation, and then only among ranch people. Most of the book deals with the history of the meat-packing industry, in which Hastings first worked; and also includes stories of his years as manager for the Swenson SMS interests. About the last third of the book consists of tales such as "Little Boy's." Another highlight among stories portraying the essence of early Texas range life is "Old Gran'pa," which also appears in the Hastings book. I have always felt that *A Ranchman's Recollections* deserves much more attention among cow-book collectors than it has had. Characters such as "Little Boy" add worthwhile flavor to the legacy of the Texas cowboy.

---

APRIL AND MAY RAINS, followed by good growing weather, had made everything beautiful in the S.M.S. pastures. The turf of curly mesquite grass was like a beautiful rug, painted here and there with wild verbena, star daisies, white and yellow primroses, and the myriad coloring of West Texas flora. Branding time was on, and the S.M.S. Flat Top Mountain outfit had gone into camp at Coon Creek Tank, to begin work the next day.

"Scandalous John," the foreman and wagon boss, had been through the aggravating experience of getting an outfit together. It had been no trouble to find riders—cowboys who knew the game from start to finish—but to secure a cook, a "hoss wrangler" and a hoodlum wagon driver was a problem. No one wants to drive the hoodlum wagon, with the duties of supplying wood and water for camp and branding, helping the cook with his dishes or other odd jobs, unprofessional, from a cowboy standpoint, except so far as they lead to a "riding job," meaning regular cowboy work. The "hoss wrangler" was not hard to find, but whoever takes the job aches all the time to be promoted to a riding job, and is therefore dissatisfied. The hoodlum driver had worked one day, and quit. Scandalous was racking his brain to know where to look for another, and was saddling his horse to hunt for one when Four-Six, one of the cowboys, exclaimed, "Look what's comin'!"

Along the dim pasture road, miles from any dwelling, a figure on foot was approaching—a sight which always attracts attention in the big pasture country, since it is associated in the public mind with suspicion, if the footman is unknown. It often occurs that some one's horse will get away or give out. The rider then makes for the nearest cow camp to borrow a horse; but a man walking needs some explanation, although he is always fed without question. The boys were all quiet and indifferent, as they commonly are in a cow camp when a stranger approaches.

A lad of sixteen, rather the worse for wear, clad in a shirt and ducking trousers, badly frayed, a soft felt hat, full of holes, shoes badly run down at the heels, and bare toes showing through the uppers, stopped within ten feet of the wagon. Scandalous paused in his saddle to say, "Well, son, in trouble?"

The lad's face, lit up by a broad grin, made an appeal to the whole outfit, and all were at attention for his answer. "No, I'm looking for the S.M.S. boss. They told me at the ranch house that he was here, and I'm looking for a job."

"You look hungry, son; come eat, an' then tell us all about it," said Scandalous.

As the lad ate, and refilled his plate and cup, the cook ventured, "Son, you're plumb welcome, but when did you eat last?"

"Night before last," the boy replied. "The brakies give me some bread and meat, but I sure was gittin ready to eat when I smelt your grub cookin down the road."

"Where be you from, son?"

"I'm from Virginia," came the reply, "and I'm sure glad to get here, and get a job."

"Virginia! A job?" exclaimed Scandalous. "How did you get here, an' how do you know you kin get a job?"

Again that good-natured grin appeared as the lad told his story.

"I walked some, and rode with the brakies some; they was mighty good to me, and give me a card to other brakies; sometimes they'd give me food they cooked in the caboose, and sometimes they took me home. I told them I was coming to the big S.M.S. Ranch to work. I worked on farms some, but hurried as much as I could, to be here branding time. Am I in time?"

The quiet assurance of the boy staggered Scandalous, but he recovered to ask, "How did you know about the S.M.S. Ranch? What made you think you could git a job? Ever done any cow work?"

The lad's grin broadened as he answered: "Well, a feller I worked for down in Virginia had one of them picture books about the S.M.S. Ranch, and I read where it said, 'No use to write for a job,' so I just cum. I kin do anything I start out to do; and I wanted to work on a ranch ever since I was a little feller; I can learn to do anything you want done, and I sure am going to work for you."

Scandalous blinked again, and said, "Why, son, we would hev' to hev' permission from your pa and ma, even if we had a job, 'cause you might git hurt."

A shade of sadness swept for a moment over the young face; then it shone again with a new light of conviction.

"I ain't got no pa or ma, I been in the orphan asylum until two years ago, when a fine man, the one with the book, took me on his farm to do chores. I didn't run away from him, neither; he said I was so crazy about comin' I'd better start. I been on the road so long the things he give me wore out. I guess I walked about a month. They told me in town to go to the office, but I was afraid they'd turn me down, so I cum to camp, and I'm a-going to stay and work for nothing."

There is a straight path to the hearts of cowboys, if one knows the way, and Scandalous was glad to hear the chorus from the whole outfit, "Let him stay Scandalous. We'll help him. Give the little boy a job."

"Reckon you kin drive the hoodlum wagon, 'Little Boy,'" said John, and, like a flash, came this response: "I don't know what a hoodlum wagon is, but I kin drive it."

It was settled. "Little Boy" was hired, and "made good." Every moment that he could get from his work found him in the branding pen, and, as is the custom with cowboys in their work, he often rode big calves. The boys, watching his skill, would get him to pull off "stunts" for visiting cowmen, until it began to be noised about that "Little Boy" in the S.M.S. outfit "was sum calf-rider." Then came the proud day of his life, when an older man was found for the hoodlum wagon. The horse wrangler was promoted to a riding job, and "Little Boy" to horse wrangler.

The boys had from the outset contributed shirts and socks; ducking trousers had been cut off for a makeshift. The first month's wages had provided a fair outfit, including the much-coveted white shirts that cowboys love to have in their "war bags" for special occasions. Succeeding months brought saddle, bridle, spurs, horse blanket and a "hot roll." "Little Boy" was coming on, but had to content himself with shoes until he had all the major necessities, and could acquire the two grand luxuries: a $15 John B. hat and $35 hand-made stitched top boots.

All through the summer "Little Boy" progressed, first from calves to yearlings in his play time, and then to outlaw broncs, until the boys in the outfit would say, "Thet kid sure kin ride; I'll bet he gets inside the money this fall at the Stamford rodeo."

Anything pertaining to an outlaw horse or steer becomes current gossip in the big pasture country, where horses and cattle form the basis of conversation about the wagon after working hours. Strange stories drifted in about a certain outlaw speckled yearling on the Lazy 7 Ranch—he had thrown every boy with rodeo aspirations who had tried to ride him, and seemed to be getting better all the time. The "Speckled Yearling" was tall, gaunt and quick as a cat. He had a mixed jump and weave that got his men about the third jump, but the boys on the Lazy 7 were keeping him to themselves, with a view to pulling off a prize "stunt" at the Stamford rodeo in September. All the little country towns held rodeos during the summer, with calf and goat roping, bronc busting and steer riding, but the big event was to come, and the boys were getting ready for it. "Little Boy" had a heart-to-heart talk with his boss, and received permission to ride steers, and tackle the "Speckled Yearling" if opportunity permitted.

At last the time for the great event came. Cowboys from 100 miles around were on hand. Professionals were barred. It was to be an event for boys who were in actual service on ranches. The S.M.S. headquarters office was thrown open for all, and the Stamford Inn pulled off an old-time cowboy dance, with old-fashioned "squares" called by old-time punchers with old-time fiddlers doing the music. The weatherman had done his best; some 2,000 people filled the grandstand, cheering the events of the first day, with now and then a call for the "Speckled Yearlin'," which was not mentioned in the programme.

Anyone who has not seen an unprofessional rodeo knows little of real cowboy sport, since it differs in its wild abandon, grace and skill from the staged events. As each favored son came on for his "stunt," he was cheered to the echo, and usually he pulled some original antic which sent the crowd wild.

The announcer, riding before the grandstand, waved for silence. "Listen people: I want you to hear this; it's a surprise, and the big event. No one has ever been able to stay ten jumps on the "Speckled Yearlin'," from the Lazy 7 Ranch. Nig Clary will now 'ride it' the Speckled Yearlin' on his own risk: A $50 prize if he stays on; a $25 forfeit if he gets throwed. If he rides him down, a hat collection will be took. If Nig can't ride him some other feller gets a chance tomorrow."

"If Nig can't nobody kin," shouted the grandstand. "Turn him a-loose." A wave from the judges' hands, and, like the cutting off of an electric current, all was still and tense. Then from the mounting chute shot the "Speckled Yearlin'," with Nig Clary up, clinging by two hand-holds to a surcingle and riding bare-back. The yearling was dead-red, with distinct white speckles about the size of one's thumb distributed well over his body. He carried long, sharp horns; his back was on the order of an Arkansas razorback hog. When it came to jumping and weaving his body at the same time, the "Speckled Yearlin'" was the limit.

*Early photograph of western artist Joe DeYong* (author's collection)

Nig sat straight for three jumps, began to wabble in the fourth and was on the ground at the fifth. Still jumping, the yearlin' turned and made for him, giving Nig only time by a scratch to climb up behind one of the judges.

The second day found "Little Boy" and Scandalous with their heads together. "I know I kin ride him, John, an' I sure want that prize money for my boots and my John B. They's all I'm needin' to be a real cowboy."

"Yes, I know," said John, "but we're needin' live cowboys, an' I ain't feelin' right 'bout your tryin' that yearlin'. I'll hev to ask you to waive all blame fer the company, an' if you do git hurt they'll be blamin' me; but if you be bound to ride, us boys will pay the forfeit, if you get throwed."

Again on the second day the announcer waved his hand for silence. "Folks, yesterday the best rider and cowpuncher in Texas rode at the speckled yearlin'. Today "Little Boy" from Flat Top Mountain Ranch says he's goin' to ride him. We hates to let a little orphan boy go agin this here steer, but he sez he ain't a-goin' to git hurt, an' if he does there ain't anybody but him. The management hopes he wins. If he does, git your change ready for a hat prize, an' I am a-goin' to start it with a five."

As boy and steer came out of the chute, the stillness fairly hurt. Every heart in that great crowd seemed to stop for the first three jumps, but "Little Boy" was sitting tight. From the crowd there came a mighty roar: "Stay with him 'Little Boy'! He's got a booger on him. Ride him 'Little Boy'!"

At the tenth jump "Little Boy" was still up, his grin growing broader and his seat getting steadier, while the yearling, maddened by his clinging burden, pitched and weaved, but, like Sinbad's "Old Man of the Sea," "Little Boy" kept a-ridin'.

The crowd went daft. Everyone was standing and shouting. The noise seemed to infuriate the yearling, and, turning from the end of the enclosure, he made straight for the grandstand, struck his head against the protecting wire, stood stock still, and glared, while "Little

Boy" sat and grinned. Some one cried "Speech!" and, as stillness came, "Little Boy," still sitting on the dazed steer, broadened his grin and said "I jest had to ride him. I needed them boots and thet John B., so's I could be a real cowboy, an' this yere speckled yearlin's done done it."

# CHAPTER VI

# ANDY ADAMS

THE STORY THAT FOLLOWS is from Andy Adams's *The Log of a Cowboy*. It is the best-known book on cowboy history ever written, if you dismiss Owen Wister's *The Virginian,* which had very little to do with cow country reality. J. Frank Dobie said of the Adams book: "If all other books on trail-driving were destroyed, a reader could still get a just and authentic conception of trail men, trail work, range cattle, cow horses, and the cow country in general from *The Log of a Cowboy.*"

Andy Adams was a prototype of the Texas cowboy. The experiences he had on the drive from the Rio Grande to the Canadian line, which are related in this book, were common to the hundreds of other Texas punchers who followed the longhorn trails. The atmosphere of life on the trail is captured by Adams with gusto and flavor. The characters, from Lovell who owned the cattle; Flood, the trail boss; and on down to Billy Honeyman, the horse wrangler, are all faithfully drawn and reflections of reality, rather than literary creations.

The story offered here constitutes a primer on the makeup of a trail outfit and details the international implications involved in putting together many of the herds that followed the

From *The Log of a Cowboy,* by Andy Adams, published by Houghton, Mifflin and Company, 1903. Reprinted with permission of Houghton, Mifflin and Company.

trails north out of Texas. The adventure of crossing the Mexican cattle to the Texas side of the Rio Grande is thrilling without the contrived drama of gunsmoke which generally characterizes cowboy novels.

The excitement and anticipation of beginning a grand adventure sets the mood for this story. The prospects of months on the trail for a young Texas cowboy, such as Adams, promised adventure enough for a lifetime for most men. The feeling was not unlike that felt by the common sailors on early Spanish voyages of discovery, nor the hunting voyages of New England whaling men.

Adams published six other books, in addition to *The Log of a Cowboy,* during his lifetime. *Cattle Brands,* published in 1906, contains one of the best of all short stories on the longhorn era, "The Story of the Poker Steer."

*The Log of a Cowboy* is a contribution of singular importance to the history of the range country. Any book on Texas cowboy bibliography which fails to consider Adams's work would be incomplete.

---

IT WAS A NICE TEN DAYS' TRIP from the San Antonio to the Rio Grande River. We made twenty-five to thirty miles a day, giving the saddle horses all the advantage of grazing on the way. Rather than hobble, Forrest night-herded them, using five guards, two men to the watch of two hours each.

"As I have little hope of ever rising to the dignity of foreman," said our segundo, while arranging the guards, "I'll take this occasion to show you varmits what an iron will I possess. With the amount of help I have, I don't propose to even catch a night horse; and I'll give the cook orders to bring me a cup of coffee and a cigarette before I arise in the morning. I've been up the trail before and realize that this authority is short-lived, so I propose to make the most of it while it lasts. Now you all know your places, and see you don't incur your foreman's displeasure."

The outfit reached Brownsville on March 25th, where we picked up Flood and Lovell, and dropping down the river about six miles below Fort Brown, went into camp at a cattle ford known as Paso Ganado. The Rio Grande was two hundred yards wide at this point, and at its then stage was almost swimming from bank to bank. It had very little current, and when winds were favorable the tide from the Gulf ran in above the ford. Flood had spent the past two weeks across the river, receiving and road-branding the herd, so when the cattle should reach the river on the Mexican side we were in honor bound to accept everything bearing the "circle dot" on the left hip. The contract called for a thousand she cattle, three and four years of age, and two thousand four and five year old beeves, estimated as sufficient to fill a million-pound beef contract. For fear of losses on the trail, our foreman had accepted fifty extra head of each class, and our herd at starting would number thirty-one hundred head. They were coming up from ranches in the interior, and we expected to cross them the first favorable day after their arrival. A number of different rancheros had turned in cattle in making up the herd, and Flood reported them in good, strong condition.

The next morning after going into camp, the first thing was the allotment of our mounts for the trip. Flood had the first pick, and cut twelve bays and browns. His preference for solid colors, though they were not the largest in the remuda, showed his practical sense of horses. When it came the boys' turn to cut, we were only allowed to cut one at a time by turns, even casting lots for first choice. We had ridden the horses enough to have a fair idea as to their merits, and every lad was his own judge. There were, as it happened, only three pinto horses in the entire bunch. Now a little boy or girl, and many an older person, thinks that a spotted horse is the real thing, but practical cattle men know that this freak of color in range-bred horses is the result of in-and-in breeding, with consequent physical and mental deterioration. It was my good fortune that morning to get a good mount of horses—three sorrels, two grays, two coyotes, a black, a brown, and a grulla. The black was my second pick, and though the color is not a hardy one, his "bread basket" indicated that he could carry food for a long ride, and ought to be a good swimmer. My judgment of him was confirmed throughout the trip, as I used him for my night horse and when we had swimming rivers to ford. I gave this black the name of "Nigger Boy."

For the trip each man was expected to furnish his own accoutrements. In saddles, we had the ordinary Texas make, the housing of which covered our mounts from withers to hips, and would weigh from thirty to forty pounds, bedecked with the latest in the way of trimmings and trappings. Our bridles were in keeping with the saddles, the reins as long as plough lines, while the bit was frequently ornamental and costly. The indispensable slicker, a greatcoat of oiled canvas, was ever at hand, securely tied to our cantle strings. Spurs were a matter of taste. If a rider carried a quirt, he usually dispensed with spurs, though, when used, those with large, dull rowels were the make commonly chosen. In the matter of leggings, not over half our outfit had any, as a trail herd always kept in the open, and except for night herding they were too warm in summer.

Either Flood or Lovell went into town every afternoon with some of the boys, expecting to hear from the cattle. On one trip they took along the wagon, laying in a month's supplies. One evening, on their return from Brownsville, Flood brought word that the herd would camp that night within fifteen miles of the river. At daybreak Lovell and the foreman, with "Fox" Quarternight and myself, started to meet the herd. The nearest ferry was at Brownsville, and it was eleven o'clock when we reached the cattle. The cattle were well shed and in good flesh for such an early season of the year, and in receiving, our foreman had been careful and had accepted only such as had strength for a long voyage. They were the long-legged, long-horned Southern cattle, pale-colored as a rule, possessed the running powers of a deer, and in an ordinary walk could travel with a horse. They had about thirty vaqueros under a corporal driving the herd, and the cattle were strung out in regular trailing manner. We rode with them until the noon hour, when, with the understanding that they were to bring the herd to Paso Ganado by ten o'clock the following day, we rode for Matamoros. Lovell had other herds to start on the trail that year, and was very anxious to cross the cattle the following day, so as to get the weekly steamer which left Port Isabel for Galveston on the first of April.

The next morning was bright and clear, with an east wind, which insured a flood tide in the river. On first sighting the herd that morning, we made ready to cross them as soon as they reached the river. The wagon was moved up within a hundred yards of the ford, and a substantial corral of ropes was stretched. Then the entire saddle stock was driven in, so as to be at hand in case a hasty change of mounts was required. By this time Honeyman knew the horses of each man's mount, so all we had to do was to sing out our horse, and Billy would have a rope on one and have him at hand before you could unsaddle a tired one. On account of our linguistic accomplishments, Quarternight and I were to be sent across the river to put the cattle in and otherwise assume control. On the Mexican side there was a single string of high brush fence on the lower side of the ford, commencing well out in the water and running back about two hundred yards, thus giving us a half chute in forcing the cattle to take swimming water.

When the herd was within a mile of the river, Fox and I shed our saddles, boots, and surplus clothing and started to meet it. The water was chilly, but we struck it with a shout, and with the cheers of our outfit behind us, swam like smugglers. A swimming horse needs freedom, and we scarcely touched the reins, but with one hand buried in a mane hold, and giving gentle slaps on the neck with the other, we guided our horses for the other shore. I was proving out my black, Fox had a gray of equal barrel displacement—both good swimmers; and on reaching the Mexican shore, we dismounted and allowed them to roll in the warm sand.

Flood had given us general instructions, and we halted the herd about half a mile from the river. The Mexican corporal was only too

*Gathered for some chuck* (author's collection)

glad to have us assume charge, and assured us that he and his outfit were ours to command. I at once proclaimed Fox Quarternight, whose years and experience outranked mine, the "gringo" corporal for the day, at which the vaqueros smiled, but I noticed they never used the word. On Fox's suggestion the Mexican corporal brought up his wagon and corralled his horses as we had done, when his cook, to our delight, invited all to have coffee before starting. That cook won our everlasting regards, for his coffee was delicious. We praised it highly, where-upon the corporal ordered the cook to have it at hand for the men in the intervals between crossing the different bunches of cattle. A March day on the Rio Grande with wet clothing is not summer, and the vaqueros hesitated a bit before following the example of Quarternight and myself and dispensing with saddles and boots. Five men were then detailed to hold the herd as compact as possible, and the remainder, twenty-seven all told, cut off about three hundred head and started for the river. I took the lead, for though cattle are less gregarious by nature than other animals, under pressure of excitement they will follow a leader. It was about noon and the herd were thirsty, so when we reached the brush chute, all hands started them on a run for the water. When the cattle were once inside the wing we went rapidly, four vaqueros riding outside the fence to keep the cattle from turning the chute on reaching swimming water. The leaders were crowding me close when Nigger breasted the water, and closely followed by several lead cattle, I struck for the American shore. The vaqueros forced every hoof into the river, following and shouting as far as the midstream, when they were swimming so nicely, Quarternight called off the men and all turned their horses back to the Mexican side. On landing opposite the exit from the ford, our men held the cattle as they came out, in order to bait the next bunch.

I rested my horse only a few minutes before taking the water again, but Lovell urged me to take an extra horse across, so as to have a change in case my black became fogged in swimming. Quarternight was a harsh segundo, for no sooner had I reached the other bank than he cut off the second bunch of about four hundred and started them. Turning Nigger Boy loose behind the brush fence, so as to be out of the way, I galloped out on my second horse, and meeting the cattle, turned and again took the lead for the river. My substitute did not swim with the freedom and ease of the black, and several times cattle swam so near me that I could lay my hands on their backs. When about halfway over, I heard shouting behind me in English, and on looking back saw Nigger Boy swimming after us. A number of vaqueros attempted to catch him, but he outswam them and came out with the cattle; the excitement was too much for him to miss.

Every trip was a repetition of the former, with varying incident. Every hoof was over in less than two hours. On the last trip, in which there were about seven hundred head, the horse of one of the Mexican vaqueros took cramps, it was supposed, at about the middle of the river, and sank without a moment's warning. A number of us heard the man's terrified cry, only in time to see horse and rider sink. Every man within reach turned to the rescue, and a moment later the man rose to the surface. Fox caught him by the shirt, and, shaking the water out of him, turned him over to one of the other vaqueros, who towed him back to their own side. Strange as it may appear, the horse never came to the surface again.

After a change of clothes for Quarternight and myself, and rather late dinner for all hands, there yet remained the counting of herd. The Mexican corporal and two of his men had come over for the purpose, and though Lovell and several wealthy rancheros, the sellers of the cattle, were present, it remained for Flood and the corporal to make the final count, as between buyer and seller. There was also present a river guard—sent out by the United States Custom House, as a matter of form in the entry papers—who also insisted on counting. In order to have a second count on the herd, Lovell ordered The Rebel to count opposite the government's man. We strung the cattle out, now logy with water, and after making quite a circle, brought the herd around where there was quite a bluff bank of the river. The herd hand led well, and in a quarter of an hour we lined them between our four mounted counters. The only difference in the manner of counting between Flood and the Mexican corporal was that the American used a tally string tied to the pommel of his saddle, on which were ten knots, keeping count by slipping a knot on each even hundred, while the Mexican used ten small pebbles, shifting a pebble from one hand to the other on hundreds.

When the count ended only two of the men agreed on numbers, The Rebel and the corporal making the same thirty-one hundred and five—Flood being one under and the Custom House man one over. Lovell at once accepted the count of Priest and the corporal; and the delivery, which, as I learned during the interpreting that followed, was to be sealed with a supper that night in Brownsville, was consummated. Lovell was compelled to leave us, to make the final payment for the herd, and we would not see him again for some time. They were all seated in the vehicle ready to start for town, when the cowman said to his foreman—

"Now, Jim, I can't give you any pointers on handling a herd, but you have until the 10th day of September to reach the Blackfoot Agency. An average of fifteen miles a day will put you there on time, so don't hurry. I'll try to see you at Dodge and Ogalalla on the way. Now, live well, for I like your outfit of men. Your credit letter is good anywhere you need supplies, and if you want more horses on the trail, buy them and draft on me through your letter of credit. If any of your men meet with accident or get sick, look out for them the same as you would for yourself, and I'll honor all the bills. And don't be stingy over your expense account, for if that herd don't make money, You and I had better quit cows."

I had been detained to do any interpreting needful, and at parting Lovell beckoned to me. When I rode alongside the carriage, he gave me his hand and said—

"Flood tells me to-day that you're a brother of Bob Quirk. Bob is to be foreman of my herd that I'm putting up in Nueces County. I'm glad you're here with Jim, though, for it's a longer trip. Yes, you'll get all the circus there is, and stay for the concert besides. They say God is good to the poor and the Irish; and if that's so, you'll pull through all right. Good-by, son." And as he gave me a hearty, ringing grip of the hand, I couldn't help feeling friendly toward him, Yankee that he was.

# CHAPTER VII

# JACK POTTER

JACK POTTER CALLED THIS STORY "Stepping High." It appeared in his little pamphlet, *Cattle Trails of the Old West,* which was privately printed at Clayton, New Mexico, in 1935 in an edition of 200 copies. Potter was a native son of the Lone Star State and made his first trip up the cattle trail in 1880 to Dodge City, Kansas.

The writings of Jack Potter comprise one other pamphlet, *Lead Steer and Other Tales,* an essay in *The Trail Driver of Texas,* and a few scattered newspaper and magazine articles. The two pamphlets deserve a special place in any comprehensive range history collection. No Texas cowboy has written of his experiences with more vitality and vigor than Potter. His stories are brimming with the flavor of cowboy life. They give the reader a sense of reality that cannot be found in all of the books written by historians who have attempted to chronicle the life and times of the cowboy.

"Stepping High" offers a delightful look at the young Texas cowboy following his first trip up the cattle trail. His adventures with his trunk, the gaslights in the hotel room, and the cowpunchers' stampede on the train are classic vignettes in cowboy literature.

From *Cattle Trails of the Old West,* by Jack Potter, published by the author, 1935.

Most of Potter's writings are quite difficult to find today. I think that a new book gathering all of his pieces would be a valuable addition to range bibliography. "Stepping High" provides abundant evidence of Potter's significance as a cowboy author. He was a friend of Texas's two top range country writers, J. Evetts Haley and J. Frank Dobie. On one occasion, he playfully considered changing his name to J. Burro Potter, since he had himself been "accused of being an author."

---

IN 1882, after trailing as a hand from the Coast of Texas to Cheyenne, Wyoming, with a herd of longhorns, I sold my mount and was left in Greeley, Colorado, our headquarters, afoot.

I couldn't help but feel I had made a mistake as I could have ridden back to Texas on horseback in forty days' time and kept from learning to ride on one of those trains.

My money bothered me considerable, and I said to myself, "If they take it away from me they'll have to strip me to do it." With that I stuck a few bills into the corner of my pocketbook, counted what I had left, folded my wage check for 150 bucks in with it, pulled out my shirt tail and tied my pocketbook hard and fast in one corner; then, stuffing it deep inside my pants, I stepped across the street and bought a plum good spotted tin trunk and 200 feet of calf rope.

Shouldering it to the depot, I dumped in my old apple tree saddle, forty-five gun, a camp sugan, hen-skin blanket and a change of dirty underwear. I shut down the lid and started roping it. Just as I was tying the last knot the boys rode up. They had come in from the ranch to see me off. One of them remarked that I had ought to get a job roping trunks for the railroad company instead of wasting my time with steers. Another boy asked why I didn't cut the rope and use less. The first suggestion I accepted in good faith; but, with a sort of contemptuous pity for the ignorance of the other boy, I said, "No, not me; nobody's going through my trunk for want of a few feet of rope."

The New England Company had given me a ticket to Denver and a letter to the ticket agent instructing him to sell me a ticket to Dodge City at reduced rates, and arrange for me to get a cowboy ticket from there to San Antonio for $25. When the 4 o'clock Union Pacific train whistled, I shook hands with the boys and one of 'em shoved a trunk check at me, saying "Your baggage is loaded. So long, Cowboy; write when you hit Texas." I climbed aboard as the train pulled out and was just getting settled, when the conductor asked for my ticket. I handed it to him and watched him punch a hole in it and another to match in a piece of red pasteboard, which he stuck in my hatband, and start on. I jumped up and yelled at him, "Here! You can't come that on me! Give me back that ticket." But if he heard me, he didn't pay heed. The train was loping ahead, and I had on my high-heeled boots, fine for riding, but no account for walking on a rollicky train; so I sat down quicker'n I expected to, and started figuring how to get my ticket back.

Just then we went over a bridge, but I saw it comin' and dodged it, got a breath and here come another. Seemed like from there to Denver about all I did was duck bridges. When we pulled into the Union Station, me feeling some lucky I hadn't been bridge scalped, I went on a still-hunt for my trunk. Not finding it, I was getting all worked up, when I saw a man loading it onto a truck. Stepping lively, I said, "I'll take that trunk." He didn't look up, nor stop loading; just said, sort of off-handed, "We're handling this baggage."

"But that's my trunk and I want it, my saddle and my gun are in it!" I fired back, getting considerably hot and bothered as I followed him into the baggage room. When we got there, with me bringing plenty of pressure to bear, a fellow at a desk laughed and said, "All right, Cowboy, give me your check and you can have it." Knowing that if I had such a thing it was bound to be tied up in my shirt-tail, along with my money, I went after it and handed him my draft for wages. Glancing at it, he handed it back with, "This isn't it. Where's the metal check with numbers on it?" Then it dawned on me what

*To Jack Potter, riding a train is more of a challenge than roping and branding calves* (National Cowboy Hall of Fame)

the cowboy had given me when he said goodbye, at Greeley, and I passed it over. He cut his eyes at it and said, "Where are you going from here, young man?" "To San Antonio, Texas," I said, "if I can ever get there." "Well, you will, all right; just leave that rope shipment here with us; we'll take care of it until you're ready to recheck, then we'll do that and load it on the train, too."

That sounded bully to me; so I struck out down town to find a place to sleep. After arranging for a room at the St. Charles hotel, I went looking for a barber shop, to get shaved, shined and shingled, and when the barber and bootblack had done all they could do for me, the barber said, "Like to have a bath?" "Yes," I said, "I shore would." I followed him down a hall to a side room, where he turned on the water over the tub, left some towels and disappeared. I hurriedly undressed, fearing the tub would run over before I got into it. Seeing the water was close to the top, I plunged in most up to my neck, let out a regular commanche war-whoop, came out on all fours and fell sprawling onto the slick, marble floor, raising a big bump on my head, where it struck the edge of the tub. "Jack Potter," I said, "you're nothing else but scalded, hog killin' fashion!" The water was running level with the top of the tub, and with no idea how to handle 'em, but knowing something had to be done, I grabbed both faucets and twisted hard. Relieved to see the water quit running, I pulled a lock of hair to see if it would slip, fanned with my Stetson to cool off, and examined my toenails, knowing they had dipped longer and deeper than the rest of me; but they still hung on.

Satisfied that I was cleaner than I'd ever been before in my life, I eased into my clothes and sauntered down the street, like cities and baths were everyday occurrences in my young life.

That night, after taking in the sights with a cowboy I met up with, I went to the hotel. The porter showed me to my room, lit the gas, asked if that would be all, and stood around a minute after I told him I couldn't see anything else for him to do. Seeing he was in no hurry to go and kept playing with the windows, letting them up, and things like that, made me sorter nervous about the money tied up in my shirt-tail; but I never let on and directly I said, "Well I'm going to bed now; you'd better go back I reckon." And he went. I felt much better, stripped for bed, and tried to blow out the gas. Failing, I fanned it with my hat, but didn't get anywhere with it, so turned in, pulled my hat down over my eyes and told the blamed gas to burn all night, for all I cared. Believe it or not, that's what it did, and when I got better acquainted with it I was nothing else but glad I hadn't blown it out, for plenty of people who did never wake up the next morning.

All set for Dodge City the next day, I hunted up my trunk. I re-checked it and picked it up to carry it to the train. But the same nice man who had watched it all night for me told me to rest easy; he would see to it; so I wandered around, not seeming to be keeping an eye on it; but I was, for fear he might let it slip him, until I saw it loaded. Then I got aboard and settled myself for a good ride. Next thing I knew I was ducking bridges again; seemed like it was going to be worse then before, and I tried to figure why folks would rather watch for them than ride a good pony. Directly, a nice looking old gentleman said, "Young man, I judge you are a typical cowboy. Doubtless you can master a broncho or rope and tie a steer in record time; but riding a train seems to be new to you. If you will turn your seat with the back toward the engine, the bridges will not disturb you." I did, and it worked fine. At midnight we pulled into Dodge City, the town that never slept, and me with a 24-hour layover.

I didn't intend to waste any of it, either; so I went to the big dance hall and got in just in time to see a cowboy and a gambler mix six-shooter bullets with plenty of smoke and stampede; but nobody was killed. Next morning the town was full of cattlemen and cowboys. I met George Saunders, late president of the Old Trail Drivers' Association, but then a roistering cowboy like myself, along with Slim Johnson, Jesse Presnall and others from Texas.

Jesse said, "Jack, old Smith and his outfit are here from Cotulla; they'll be in directly; figuring on going back tonight. He's one of the best trail men that ever drove a cow; but he's all worked up about having to ride the cushions home. Wish you'd help 'em change cars down the line and sorter look after 'em." About 4 o'clock here comes a chuck wagon, loaded with punchers and headed by Smith. That night we visited every saloon in town. At 1 o'clock I saw a Texas cowman lose a whole herd of cattle on the turn of a card, without batting an eye, but he may have won them back before daylight.

When the train pulled in, Smith and his bunch stampeded, and it took all hands and the cook to get 'em aboard. I knew exactly how they felt, and while I was feeling some better than when I left Greeley, I wasn't easy in my mind on a railroad train. At 12:30 I gave the conductor my cowboy ticket, long as my arm. He looked at it and saw it was all right. As he tore off a chunk, I said, "What right have you to tear up a man's ticket?" He laughed and said, "You're on my division. I tore off one coupon, and every conductor between here and San Antonio will do the same thing."

It sounded all right, but I was worried for fear my ticket would not hold out until I got home. We bedded down, and at 3 o'clock they side-tracked us to let the west-bound passenger go by. When it came whizzing along we were sleeping like the dead. Just as the locomotive got even with our car it let out a shrill whistle. Talk about your stampedes! Boy, we had it. Those sleepy cowboys rose as one man off to a run, with old Smith leading the herd. I was a little slow in getting off, but I fell in with the "drags," and half asleep, I thought I was in a sure enough cattle stampede; so I went to yelling, "Circle your leaders and keep up the drags!"

They circled all right, knocked some of us down, and circled again. The news butch crawled from under a seat and went through the window, sash and all. The train crew pushed through the door, caught old Smith and quieted things down. The conductor was mad as a hornet and threatened to put us into a stock car. We held court next day, and when one of the "brakies" said it was a trick of the engineer to whistle at that siding, and that he undoubtedly had caused many a stampede, the jury returned a verdict of guilty, with the death penalty, by capturing and hog-tying him on the Western Trail, road-branding him with a hot iron and letting 5,000 longhorns stampede on top of him.

We met up with some fine girls, whose folks were moving to

Uvalde, and they entertained us until we changed cars at Taylor, Texas. When we said goodbye, the one that had me locoed asked me to write in her autograph album. That was the '82 fad. We have a new one in America every year, the last more foolish than the first. That girl had me up a tree, no fooling. She kept begging, with me refusing, till finally I took the book and started writing down all the road brands I knew. She said, "Oh, write a verse of some kind!" I said, "I don't know any verse." Then, all of a sudden, I remembered part of one I learned in my school reader; so I wrote: "It's tiresome work," says lazy Ned, "to climb the hill with my new sled and beat the other boys."

Then I signed it, "Your Bully friend, Jack Potter," and handed it back. She gave it the once-over, cut her eyes at me, smiled and said, sweet as honeydripping out of the comb, "Now, that's what I call poetry, and you're my kind of man, Cowboy." Lord-a-mercy! I broke out in a big sweat, and, says I to myself, "That train had better hurry if it's going to take me along!" Girls always did flustrate me, and do yet, if my wife's not looking.

We were three months making this drive, and I worked a month on the Crow ranch before I drove some horses up to Tongue River, Montana.

I got through fine, and liked it best of anything I'd ever done, till I tied in with the train coming back. Between the bridges, riding so durned fast, worrying about my trunk and scared to death over old Smith's stampede, I was plum shot to pieces when the train porter yelled "San Antonio!" Then I led the bunch to the bed ground, with Smith swearing that Texas had the world by the tail, and me a backing him up on it.

# CHAPTER VIII

# CHARLIE SIRINGO

A TEXAS COWBOY, *or Fifteen Years on the Hurricane Deck of a Spanish Pony,* was written by Charles A. Siringo and first published in 1885. It was the first cowboy autobiography to be published and had considerable influence on other cowboys who subsequently wrote down their own stories.

Will Rogers once wrote to Siringo that *A Texas Cowboy* "was the Cowboy's Bible when I was growing up. I camped with a herd one night at the old L X Ranch, just north of Amarillo in '98, and they showed me an old forked tree where some old bronc had bucked you into. Why, that to us was like looking at the shrine of Shakespeare to some of these deep foreheads. . . ."

The value of *A Texas Cowboy* rests not only in the fact that it was the first cowboy autobiography; it is also one of the most genuine and well written of the entire genre. It is an opinion of many serious cattle book collectors that *The Texas Cowboy* and "Teddy Blue's" *We Pointed Them North* (see Chapter Nine) are the two most important of all the volumes of cowboy reminiscences.

The selection offered here is taken from the chapter "On a Tare in Wichita." Most cowboy stories deal with episodes in-

From *A Texas Cowboy, or Fifteen Years on the Hurricane Deck of a Spanish Pony,* by Charles A. Siringo, published by M. Umbdenstock and Company, 1885.

volving several men in a trail outfit or a roundup crew. This story presents the young cowboy alone and on his own in a challenging situation. His desire at the end, to "leave that God-Forsaken country in less than twenty-four hours," is a familiar feeling to all South Texas cowboys who have experienced northern winters.

*A Texas Cowboy* was written before Siringo was thirty years old. He wrote six other books covering his range experiences as well as his adventures as a Pinkerton detective. *A Texas Cowboy* is one of the two or three most important books existing on cowboy life. To own a copy of the original 1885 edition is any cow-book collector's dream.

---

O N THE FOURTH DAY OF JULY, after being on the trail just three months, we landed on the "Ninnasquaw" river, thirty miles west of Wichita, Kansas.

Nearly all the boys, the boss included, struck out for Wichita right away to take the train for Houston, Texas, the nearest railroad point to their respective homes. Mr. Grimes paid their railroad fares according to custom in those days. I concluded I would remain until fall.

Mr. Grimes had come around by rail, consequently he was on hand to receive us. He already had several thousand steers—besides our herd—on hand; some that he drove up the year before and others he had bought around there. He had them divided up into several different herds—about eight hundred to the herd—and scattered out into different places, that is each camp off by itself, from five to ten miles from any other. With each herd or bunch would be a cook and chuck wagon, four riders, a boss included—and five horses to the rider. During the day two men would "herd" or watch the cattle until noon and the other two until time to "bed" them, which would be about dark. By "bedding" we mean take them to a camp, to a certain high piece of ground suitable for a "bed ground" where they would all lie down until morning, unless disturbed by a storm or otherwise. The nights would be divided up into four equal parts—one man "on" at a time, unless storming, tormented with mosquitos or something of the kind, when everyone except the cook would have to be "out" singing to them.

The herd I came up the trail with was split into three bunches and I was put with one of them under a man by the name of Phillups, but shortly afterwards changed and put with a Mr. Taylor.

I spent all my extra time when not on duty, visiting a couple of New York damsels, who lived with their parents five miles east of our camp. They were the only young ladies in the neighborhood, the country being very thinly settled then, therefore the boys thought I was very cheeky—getting on courting terms with them so quick. One of them finally "put a head on me"—or in grammatical words, gave me a black eye—which chopped my visits short off; she didn't understand the Texas way of proposing for one's hand in marriage, was what caused the fracas. She was cleaning roasting-ears for dinner when I asked her how she would like to jump into double harness and trot through life with me? The air was full of flying roasting-ears for a few seconds—one of them striking me over the left eye— and shortly afterwards a young Cow Puncher rode into camp with one eye in a sling. You can imagine the boys giving it to me about monkeying with civilized girls, etc.

After that I became very lonesome; had nothing to think of but my little Texas girl—the only one on earth I loved. While sitting on herd in the hot sun, or lounging around camp in the shade of the wagon—there being no trees in that country to supply us with shade —my mind would be on nothing but her. I finally concluded to write to her and find out just how I stood. As often as I had been with her I had never let her know my thoughts. She being only fourteen years of age, I thought there was plenty of time. I wrote a long letter explaining everything and then waited patiently for an answer. I felt sure she would give me encouragement, if nothing more.

A month passed by and still no answer. "Can it be possible that she don't think enough of me to answer my letter?" thought I. "No,"

I would finally decide, "She is too much of an angel to be guilty of such."

At last the supply wagon arrived from Wichita and among the mail was a letter for me. I was on herd that forenoon and when the boys came out to relieve Collier and I, they told me about there being a letter in camp for me, written by a female, judging the fine hand-writing on the envelope.

I was happy until I opened the letter and read a few lines. It then dropped from my fingers and I turned deathly pale. Mr. Collier wanted to know if some of my relations wasn't dead? Suffice it to say that the object of my heart was married to my old playmate Billy Williams. The letter went on to state that she had given her love to another and that she never thought I loved her only as a friend, etc. She furthermore went on advising me to grin and bear it, as there were just as good fish in the sea as ever was caught, etc.

I wanted some one to kill me, so concluded to go to the Black hills—as everyone was flocking there then. Mr. Collier agreed to go with me. So we both struck out for Wichita to settle up with Daddy Grimes. Mr. Collier had a good horse of his own and so did I; mine was a California pony that I had given fifty-five dollars for quite awhile before. My intention was to take him home and make a race horse of him; he was only three years old and according to my views a "lightning striker."

After settling up, we, like other "locoed" Cow Punchers proceeded to take in the town, and the result was, after two or three days carousing around, we left there "busted" with the exception of a few dollars.

As we didn't have money enough to take us to the Black hills, we concluded to pull for the Medicine river, one hundred miles west.

We arrived in Kiowa, a little one-horse town on the Medicine, about dark one cold and disagreeable evening.

We put up at the Davis House, which was kept by a man named Davis—by the way one of the whitest men that ever wore shoes. Collier made arrangements that night with Mr. Davis to board us on "tick" until we could get work. But I wouldn't agree to that.

The next morning after paying my night's lodging I had just one dollar left and I gave that to Mr. Collier as I bade him adieu. I then headed southwest across the hills, not having any destination in view; I wanted to go somewhere but didn't care where—to tell the truth I was still somewhat rattled over my recent bad luck.

That night I lay out in the brush by myself and next morning changed my course to southeast, down a creek called Driftwood. About noon I accidentally landed in Gus Johnson's cow camp at the forks of Driftwood and "Little Mule" creeks.

I remained there all night and next morning when I was fixing to pull out—God only knows where, the boss, Bill Hudson, asked me if I wouldn't stay and work in his place until he went to Hutchison, Kansas and back? I agreed to do so finally if he would furnish "Whisky-peat," my pony, all the corn he could eat—over and above my wages, which were to be twenty-five dollars a month. The outfit consisted of only about twenty-five hundred Texas steers, a chuck wagon, cook, and five riders besides the boss.

A few days after Mr. Hudson left we experienced a terrible severe snow storm. We had to stay with the drifting herd night and day, therefore it went rough with us—myself especially, being from a warm climate and only clad in common garments, while the other boys were fixed for winter.

When Mr. Hudson came back from Hutchison he pulled up stakes and drifted south down into the Indian territory—our camp was then on the territory and Kansas line—in search of good winter quarters.

We located on the "Eagle Chief" river, a place where cattle had never been held before. Cattlemen in that section of country considered it better policy to hug the Kansas line on account of indians.

About the time we became settled in our new quarters, my month was up and Mr. Hudson paid me twenty-five dollars, telling me to make that my home all winter if I wished.

My "pile" now amounted to forty-five dollars, having won twenty dollars from one of the boys, Ike Berry, on a horse race. They had a race horse in camp called "Gray-dog," who had never been beaten, so

*"A cowboy, his horse and the cattle; the cast of the pageant of the open range."* (author's collection)

they said, but I and Whisky-peat done him up, to the extent of twenty dollars, in fine shape.

I made up my mind that I would build me a "dugout" some where close to the Johnson camp and put in the winter hunting and trapping. Therefore as Hudson was going to Kiowa, with the wagon, after a load of provisions, etc., I went along to lay me in a supply also.

On arriving at Kiowa I found that my old "pard" Mr. Collier had struck a job with a cattleman whose ranch was close to town. But before spring he left for good "Hold Hengland" where a large pile of money was awaiting him; one of his rich relations had died and willed him everything he had. We suppose he is not putting on lots of "agony," if not dead, and telling his green countrymen of his hair-breadth escapes on the wild Texas plains.

After sending mother twenty dollars by registered mail and lay-ing in a supply of corn, provisions, ammunition, etc., I pulled back to Eagle Chief, to make war with wild animals—especially those that their hides would bring me in some money, such as gray wolves, coyotes, wild cats, buffaloes and bears. I left Kiowa with just three dollars in money.

The next morning after arriving in camp I took my stuff and moved down the river about a mile to where I had already selected a spot for my winter quarters.

I worked like a turk all day long building me a house out of dry poles—covered with grass. In the north end I built a sod chimney and in the south end, left an opening for a door. When finished it lacked about two feet of being high enough for me to stand up straight.

It was almost dark and snowing terribly when I got it finished and a fire burning in the low, Jim Crow fire-place. I then fed Whisky-peat some corn and stepped out a few yards after an armful of good solid wood for morning. On getting about half an armful of wood gathered I heard something crackling and looking over my shoulder discovered my mansion in flames. I got there in time to save nearly everything in the shape of bedding, etc. Some of the grub, being next to the fire-place, was lost. I slept at Johnson's camp that night.

The next morning I went about two miles down the river and located another camp. This time I built a dug-out right on the bank of the stream, in a thick bunch of timber.

I made the dug-out in a curious shape; started in at the edge of the steep bank and dug a place six feet long, three deep and three wide, leaving the end next to the creek open for a door. I then commenced at the further end and dug another place same size in an opposite direction, which formed an "L." I then dug still another place, same size, straight out from the river which made the whole concern almost in the shape of a "Z." In the end furthest from the stream I made a fire-place by digging the earth away in the shape of a regular fire-place. And then to make a chimney I dug a round hole, with the aid of a butcher knife, straight up as far as I could reach; then commencing at the top and connected the two holes. The next thing was to make it "draw," and I did that by cutting and piling sods of dirt around the hole, until about two feet above the level.

I then proceeded to build a roof over my 3 x 18 mansion. To do that I cut green poles four feet long and laid them across the top, two or three inches apart. Then a layer of grass and finally, to finish it off, a foot of solid earth. She was then ready for business. My idea in making it so crooked was, to keep the indians, should they happen along at night, from seeing my fire. After getting established in my new quarters I put out quite a number of wolf baits and next morning in going to look at them found several dead wolves besides scores of skunks, etc. But they were frozen too stiff to skin, therefore I left them until a warmer day.

The next morning on crawling out to feed my horse I discovered it snowing terribly, accompanied with a piercing cold norther. I crawled back into my hole after making Whisky-peat as comfortable as possible and remained there until late in the evening, when suddenly disturbed by a horny visitor.

It was three or four o'clock in the evening, while humped up before a blazing fire, thinking of days gone by, that all at once, before I had time to think, a large red steer came tumbling down head first, just missing me by a few inches. In traveling ahead of the storm the whole Johnson herd had passed right over me, but luckily only one broke through.

Talk about your ticklish places! That was truly one of them; a steer jammed in between me and daylight, and a hot fire roasting me by inches.

I tried to get up through the roof—it being only a foot above my head—but failed. Finally the old steer made a terrible struggle, just about the time I was fixing to turn my wicked soul over to the Lord, and I got a glimpse of daylight under his flanks. I made a dive for it and by tight squeezing I saved my life.

After getting out and shaking myself I made a vow that I would leave that God-forsaken country in less than twenty-four hours; and I did so.

# CHAPTER IX

# TEDDY BLUE

E. C. ABBOTT was known as "Teddy Blue" in the cow country from Texas to Montana. His book, *We Pointed Them North,* was published over fifty years after Siringo's *A Texas Cowboy.* There were hundreds of cowboy books written during that period, yet Teddy Blue's story is the first to hit the mark set by Siringo. It is a wonderfully original treatment of a much-used theme. What sets it apart is its tone of unrestrained, devil-be-damned, full gallop. This book, as indicated by the selection offered here, gives a more thorough and faithful insight into the cowboy's life when he wasn't with the cows than any other cowboy book ever printed. Texas cowboys were not the austere, heroic characters of Zane Grey novels. They were most often young, virile men to whom life in a cow camp only partially satisfied their quest for adventure.

Abbott was born in England, but made his first trip up the Texas cattle trail as a horse wrangler when he was ten years old. As a young man he worked all over the cow country of central Montana, became a partner of Charlie Russell, and married the half-breed daughter of Montana's most promi-

From *We Pointed Them North: Recollections of a Cowpuncher,* by E. C. Abbott ("Teddy Blue") and Helena Huntington Smith. New edition copyright 1955 by the University of Oklahoma Press. Reprinted with permission of University of Oklahoma Press.

nent cattleman, Granville Stuart. In between there were plenty bad horses, wild cattle, friendly women and ample raw whiskey to occupy the attention of "the best-looking cowboy on Powder River."

Teddy Blue earned his spurs in the Texas tradition, among Texas men and Texas cattle. He wrote: ". . . the Texas cowboy's mode of speech and dress and actions set the style for all the range country. And his influence is not dead yet."

*We Pointed Them North* is a range book of merit. The story presented here is one of the very few realistic pictures we find of what cowboys did when they weren't busy being tall in the saddle.

———————

THE COWPUNCHER was a totally different class from these other fellows on the frontier. We was the salt of the earth, any way in our own estimation, and we had the pride that went with it. That was why Miles City changed so much after the trail herds got there; even the women changed. Because buffalo hunters and that kind of people would sleep with women that cowpunchers wouldn't look at, and it was on our account that they started bringing in girls from eastern cities, young girls and pretty ones.

There was three of us from the N Bar that stayed in Miles City that week, John Burgess, John Bowen, and me. Burgess and Bowen were wagon bosses, and they were a little bit older than the rest of us with the outfit; I think Burgess was twenty-seven. But their dignity didn't bother them any when they were in town. I remember some fellow come around wanting Burgess for something and he asked Zeke Newman where he was. Newman said: "If you're looking for any of them N Bar tigers, you'll find them at the parlor house."

Mag Burns' parlor house that was; on a side street, Number 44. I was at Maggie Burns' the time my singing got me in trouble and the marshal pretty nearly had me treed instead of the other way around.

*Did he dress this way for his trips to town?*
(The Dobie Collection, University of Texas, Austin)

Three of us was in the parlor of Maggie Burns' house giving a song number called "The Texas Ranger." John Bowen was playing the piano and he couldn't play the piano, and Johnny Stringfellow was there sawing on a fiddle and he couldn't play a fiddle, and I was singing, and between the three of us we was raising the roof. And Maggie —the redheaded, fighting son of a gun—got hopping mad and says: "If you leather-legged sons of bitches want to give a concert, why don't you hire a hall? You're ruinin' my piano."

So I got mad, too, and I says: "If I had little Billy here"—well, I told her what I'd do to her piano. And John Bowen said: "Go and get him, Teddy, go and get him." That was enough for me. I went across the street and got Billy out of the livery stable, and came back and rode him through the hall into the parlor, where I dismounted. And as soon as I got in the parlor, Maggie slammed the door and locked it, and called the police.

But there was a big window in the room, that was low to the ground, and Billy and me got through it and got away. We headed for the ferry on a dead run. I got to the ferry just as it was pulling out, and jumped Billy across a little piece of water onto the apron. The sheriff got there right after me and he was hollering at the ferryman to stop, and the ferryman hollered back at him: "This fellow has got a gun the size of a stovepipe stuck in my ribs, and I ain't agoing to stop."

It all blew over and I came back to Miles City the next day.

Cowboy Annie lived at Mag Burns' house. She was the N Bar outfit's girl. They were all stuck on her except the bookkeeper, the nigger cook, and me. Her pal was my sweetheart. But Cowboy Annie surely had the rest of them on her string, and that was true as long as the N Bar Outfit in that part of the country held together. She used to tickle me to death. She had a little book, with all her fellows' names written down in it, and she would say to me: "Now just make all the brands in it, Teddy." The boys wouldn't all get to town at once as a rule, but when they did there was hellapopping.

Burgess was really gone on her. I introduced them that fall in Miles City, and it lasted until she got played out and went to Fort

Assiniboine, on Milk River, to a soldier dive. She took to drinking and bad acting before that. The soldiers was the bottom. They used to say in this country that when a women left the dogs she'd go to the soldiers. But all that was quite a few years later. She was at her height in Miles City, an awful pretty girl, with dark eyes and hair. And she could work Burgess for anything.

One day she said to him, kind of coaxing, "Oh, Johnny, I've got a sealskin coat and cap coming from Chicago, and there's still $150 against it at the express office. Won't you get it out for me?"

He made some excuse—said he didn't have $150. She pouted. "I don't care. Jim Green will get it out for me." He was foreman of the S T outfit. And Johnny fell like a ton of bricks. He said: "I've got just as much money as any S T son of a gun in Montana." And he went down to the express office and got it for her.

I believe he'd have married her if she'd have had him. She could have her pick of a dozen fellows, but she didn't want any of them. I guess after the life she'd led she couldn't see living on a homestead, getting up early in the morning, working hard, having a lot of kids. The girls like her that quit and settled down was usually worn out and half dead before they did it.

There was a lot of fellows in the eighties who were glad enough to marry them, but I never would have married that kind. I always secretly had in my heart the hopes of meeting a nice girl. I always wanted a cow ranch and a wife, and I got them both. And it was hard going at times, but believe me it was worth it.

I got to talking to one of those chippies out in this country about thirty years back, about her life, and the different places she had been, and so forth. Her name was Myrtle, and her and her sister came up here to Gilt Edge for payday. Afterwards when she had more or less reformed and was running a decent rooming house in Lewistown, I stayed there one time and got to talking with her. I said: "Before I was married, I used to hop around among you folks a good deal and I don't see how you stand it. It looks like a hell of a life to me."

She said: "Well, you know there's a kind of a fascination about it. Most of the girls that are in it wouldn't leave it if they could."

Some of those girls in Miles City were famous, like Cowboy Annie and Connie the Cowboy Queen. Connie had a $250 dress embroidered with all the different brands—they said there wasn't an outfit from the Yellowstone down to the Platte, and over in the Dakotas too, that couldn't find its brand on that dress.

We all had our favorites after we got acquainted. We'd go in town and marry a girl for a week, take her to breakfast and dinner and supper, be with her all the time. You couldn't do that in other places. There was two girls I knew in Lincoln that I wanted to take to a show one night. I had to take them in a hack, because if they had walked down the street they would have been arrested. But Lincoln had a very religious mayor and was getting civilized. You couldn't walk around with those girls in the daytime like you could in Miles City.

Things were different down South, too, from what they were up North. In Texas men couldn't be open and public about their feelings towards those women, the way we were. I suppose those things would shock a lot of respectable people. But we wasn't respectable and we didn't pretend to be, which was the only way we was different from some others. I've heard a lot about the double standard, and seen a lot of it, too, and it don't make any sense for the man to get off so easy. If I'd have been a woman and done what I done, I'd have ended up in a sporting house.

I used to talk to those girls, and they would tell me a lot of stuff about how they got started, and how in Chicago and those eastern cities they wasn't allowed on the streets, how their clothes would be taken away from them, only what they needed in the house, so it was like being in prison. They could do as they pleased out here. And they were human, too. They always had money and they would lend it to fellows that were broke. The wagon bosses would come around looking for men in the spring, and when a fellow was hired he would go to his girl and say: "I've got a job, but my bed's in soak." Or his saddle or his six-shooter or his horse. And she would lend him the money to get it back and he would pay her at the end of the month. Cowboy Annie was the kind who would always dig down and help the boys out, and so were a lot of them. They always got it back. I never knew of but one case where a fellow cheated one of those girls, and I'll bet he never tried it again. He come up the trail for one of the N Bar outfits—not ours, but the one on the Niobrara—and he went with Cowboy Annie for a week. Then he got on his horse and rode away, owing her seventy dollars. First he went back to the Niobrara, but the foreman of the outfit heard of it and fired him, then he went down in Texas, but they heard of it down there and fired him again. And the N Bar fellows took up a collection and paid her what he owed, because they wouldn't have a thing like that standing against the name of the outfit.

That shows you how we were about those things. As Mag Burns used to say, the cowpunchers treated them sporting women better than some men treat their wives.

Well, they were women. We didn't know any others. And any man that would abuse one of them was a son of a gun.

I can tell you about something that happened to me one time, and the close shave I had, all because of these notions of chivalry toward women, no matter who they were. I was with a girl at a house one night—Omaha, I called her, because she said that was where she came from. This happened in Miles City, the winter I was with the F U F, and I was just twenty-three years old.

In the middle of the night we heard this fracas downstairs—a woman's screams and then something that sounded like a body falling. I thought, "Somebody's been killed, sure." And then I heard footsteps coming up the stairs. I got up and got my six-shooter and went and stood at the head of the stairs, and there was a woman coming up, slowly. She had on a white nightgown, and the front of it was all covered with blood. I found out later that it just came from a cut on her forehead. But it looked terrible. I heard someone coming behind her, and I called down: "If you take one more step, I'll shoot you." And I would have, because I thought I couldn't do less.

Well, the woman was Willie Johnson, who ran the house. She came into the room, and I helped her to get fixed up. She was in an awful mess, with blood all over her from that cut on her forehead, and a black eye that he gave her, this man who was her sweetheart.

"I don't care for the black eye, Teddy," she whimpered, "but he called me a whore."

Can you beat that? It was what she was. I was never so disgusted in my life. I was such a damn fool. I might have killed that man and got into a peck of trouble. Knight of the Plains. Had to protect all females. Lord!

But the black-eye story was another one of the things that were repeated all around, and got to be a by-word with the cowpunchers. So that when I was on herd, somebody would yell across in a high-pitched voice: "Oh, Ted-dee! I don't mind the black eye . . ." and so forth. But just the same it shows the way I felt about those women at that time. If you were good to them, they'd appreciate it, and believe me, they had ways of repaying a kindness, as I ought to know.

I always had money because I didn't gamble—only a little now and then. I couldn't see giving it to them tinhorns. You knew they were going to take it away from you. And besides, I never had time to gamble; couldn't sit still long enough! I always had to be up, talking, singing, drinking at the bar. I was so happy and full of life, I used to feel, when I got a little whisky inside me, that I could jump twenty feet in the air. I'd like to go back and feel that way once more. If I could go back I wouldn't change any part of it.

A night or two before we left town that fall, we were all together with the girls, drinking and having a good time and I got dressed up. Cowboy Annie put her gold chain around my neck, and wound her scarf around the crown of my Stetson, and this started us talking about the stunt that Jake Des Rosses pulled at Ogallala the year before. There was a dance going on and not enough women to go around, which was the usual way of it in that country, and a couple of fellows got left without a partner. So one of them said: "I'll fix that." And he went in a back room—this was a honky-tonk, of course —and he came out with a pair of woman's white ruffled drawers pulled on over his pants. He and the other fellow danced around, and it brought the house down.

So we were talking about it and Cowboy Annie turned to me. "Would you do that?" she says.

I said yes, naturally. So she pulled them off, and I put them on over my pants. And we all paraded down the street, me with my gold necklace and the trimmings on my hat and Cowboy Annie's drawers on. The whole town turned out to see us. It turned the place upside down.

Well, that was the kind of wild, crazy stunt that gave me my reputation. They'd tell about a thing like that clear down to Texas. The reps would ride around to the roundups and carry it along, and in the wintertime the grub line riders would carry it. We had to talk about something. It was all the fun we had.

Next day, or the day after that, we all left for the mouth of the Musselshell. In the morning when we was ready Burgess wasn't there. Somebody had seen his horse, with the reins dropped, standing in front of the parlor house, and I went up there to get him. He was in Cowboy Annie's room. He had been to the bank and got the money and gone back there to pay her, for the week. And when I came in—because I was a friend of them both—she flipped the pillow cover and showed me the yellow pile nested there—seventy dollars in gold.

After that, going back to the mouth of the Musselshell, I made up a song about Cowboy Annie, that went:

> *Cowboy Annie was her name,*
> *And the N Bar outfit was her game.*

and ended up:

> *And when the beef is four years old,*
> *We'll fill her pillow slips with gold.*

I still had Cowboy Annie's ruffled drawers that she gave me that night, and I put them on a forked stick and carried them that way to the mouth of the Musselshell, like a flag. And before we left, my girl took one of her stockings off and tied it around my arm, you know, like the knights of old, and I wore that to the mouth of the Musselshell.

After we got up there, I had the flag hanging on the wall of the cabin, until Harry Rutler got sore one day and tore it down and throwed it in the stove. He said it wasn't decent. And no more it was.

# CHAPTER X

# ROLLIE BURNS

THIS STORY REPRESENTS the Texas cowboy and his life in the Texas Panhandle area of the Llano Estacado. Rollie Burns's recollections were encouraged by range historian J. Evetts Haley and arranged and edited for publication by W. C. Holden, a professor at Texas Tech, in Lubbock. The Southwest Press, which also published J. Frank Dobie's first book, *A Vaquero of the Brush Country,* released *Rollie Burns* in 1932 in an edition of 500 copies. Carl Hertzog of El Paso later published 500 additional copies. The first issue has long been a much-sought-after item among collectors of cattle books.

The chapter offered here presents a marked contrast to the social activities engaged in by Teddy Blue in the previous chapter. It is not that Rollie Burns was that much different from Teddy Blue; Texas cowboys had a strict, well-defined code of conduct governing their behavior around "proper" women. The cowboys at Slaughter's Christmas ball would have behaved much differently had they been in a "parlor house" in Dodge, or Miles City. Teddy Blue would also have known how to act had he attended the Panhandle dance. There were few settlements in the early days of West Texas

From *Rollie Burns,* by W. C. Holden, published by Southwest Press, 1932. Reprinted with permission of the author.

and Panhandle ranching. The dances described by Burns accounted for almost all the relief there was from the monotony of cow work. The Texas range was being fenced in an ever-increasing volume, and the era of trail driving came to a sudden halt, barely twenty years after it had begun. Burns finally gave up life in the saddle. In later years he lamented: "As long as I stayed in the cattle business I prospered, but when I left the only vocation I knew, every venture that I made was for the worse."

———————

THE WINTER OF 1881–1882 was a gay one for the cowboys of Crosby, Floyd, Motley, Dickens, Kent, Garza, Lynn and Lubbock Counties. We had two dances, one at Will Slaughter's in January, and one at Dockum's in March. The one at Dockum's was scheduled to take place first, but had to be postponed about three months.

We were all excited about the dances, and had been for weeks. Ever since the fall round-ups were over, practically all our talk had been about the forth-coming dances. We started getting ready for Slaughter's dance a week before it began. I had brought three white shirts from home. They had been white before I left home, but hanging around in a dug out for six months had changed their color. Will Sanders, John Garrison and I conceived the idea of washing these shirts and "putting on some dog" at the dance. We didn't have any place to wash them but the creek, and the water there was of a reddish, muddy hue. We washed them all right, but when we got through the shirts were a streaked pink color.

The next day Will Sanders came by L. A. Wilson's dugout over on Pole Canyon and found a smoothing iron and about four pounds of starch. Mrs. Wilson had left these articles at the dugout the previous fall when she and her husband returned to Jacksboro. (Wilson ranged with the Hensleys, and our outfit looked after his cattle during the winter.) It had not occurred to us that we ought to starch or iron our shirts, but when Will saw that starch and smoothing iron, the idea struck him, and he came wagging them into camp, looking a little sheepish. The idea went over big with John and me, and we got busy at once. We filled one of the Dutch ovens two-thirds full of water and put in about two and one-half pounds of starch. We got it boiling and then baptized the shirts. Then we hung them out on bushes to dry. We didn't wring them any, because we didn't want to lose any of our precious starch. When they got dry, they seemed to be starched a-plenty. They were hard as boards and would stand alone. We were puzzled, then, as to how to get them ironed. One of the boys remembered seeing his mother sprinkle clothes before ironing; then we all remembered having seen that done at home. We sprinkled the shirts and they would still stand alone. We tried to put them on and failed at that. John suggested, maybe, we had used too much starch. So we made up another batch, this time putting in about half as much starch. When it got to boiling, we stuck the shirts in. They collapsed slowly like a hard lump of sugar melting at the bottom. When they dried, they would still stand alone. We didn't realize that all the starch of the first dipping was still in the shirts. We took the shirts to the creek and let them soak while we got some chuck. We had been so busy that we had let half the afternoon slip by without realizing it was time to eat. After chuck, we got ready to iron, but when we brought our shirts out they were as limber as a rawhide string that had been left in the water overnight. Will suggested that we give them another starching, but we found we had used all the starch. Then we proceeded with the ironing. The iron had rust on it, and when we finished, our shirts were a yellowish pink with brown spots from the iron all over them. We looked them over and decided it was a failure. We had spent the better part of two days and all Mrs. Wilson's starch and made a bad job of it. I suppose that if the starch and shirts had held out we would have stayed at it several days. As it was, we had to wear old cowpunchin' togs to the dance. We washed them out in the creek, but didn't attempt the ironing business on them.

The morning before the dance was to start we spent trying to shave. I had brought an old razor with me, but none of us had tried to use it since I arrived six months before. Our beards were full of grit and none of us were very good at sharpening a razor. We used the stirrup leather of a saddle for a strop. We would pull at our whiskers awhile and strop awhile. We didn't have a looking glass, so we had to shave each other. Will and I got our beards off after a fashion, but when John saw how much blood we were bringing, he decided he would go to the dance with his beard intact.

We started at noon because it was twelve miles, and we wanted to arrive early. Others were already arriving when we got there. The women were coming in buckboards and hacks, and the men on horseback. We hobbled our horses out, and got ready for supper.

Will Slaughter had gotten ready for us in big style. He had barbecued a beef, had boiled a bunch of hams (of wild hogs), had roasted several turkeys, had several quarters of venison ready to cut into steaks, and antelope meat ready to be made into stew with "sinkers" (dumplings). Mrs. Slaughter had made several gallons of jelly and preserves from wild plums during the previous summer. She had cooked a tub full of doughnuts, stacks of fried apple pies, and some cakes—the first I had seen since I left home. The coffee pot was kept steaming until we left three days later.

There were nine women present. Mrs. Will Slaughter, Mrs. Sam Gholson and her two daughters from the extreme southeast corner of Lubbock County, Mrs. Coon Cooper from Garza County, Miss Scarborough from Snyder, and Miss Rodie DeGraffenried from Dickens County. There were so many cowboys they couldn't get in the house at the same time; there were thirty or more. About dark George Edwards got out his fiddle and started tuning up. He thumped, twisted, listened, strummed, and sawed for a half hour. I couldn't see that he was making much headway, but he finally got it fixed to suit him and drew the bow vigorously across the strings a few times by way of warming up. Then Bill Petty, a six-footer with a pair of leather lungs from the Spur range on Red Mud, bellowed, "Get yer partners fer the first dance."

*After this kind of work, dancing and drinking are well-earned re-wards* (National Cowboy Hall of Fame)

Most of the boys were kinda shy at first. They had not been around women for so long that they were a little afraid of them. Enough of the more brazen ones got up sufficient courage to ask partners for the first dance. Two rooms had been cleared for dancing. They were so small that only one set could dance in each room at a time. The fiddler sat in the clear between the two rooms.

When four couples had gotten out on the floor, George Edwards struck up a tune and started keeping time energetically with his bootheel.

Three nights and two days—quadrilles, waltzes, schottisches, and polkas. I wondered how the women stood it. With the men it was different. There were three times as many of them as women; consequently they got to rest about two-thirds of the time. When one of the boys got tired and sleepy, he could go out to the half dugout used for a bunk house and get a nap, but the women were not given much chance to rest. However, they danced with minimum exertion. The men swung them so lustily that little effort was necessary on their part. Before daybreak of the third morning, however, their feet got tired and sore.

A considerable amount of whiskey was in evidence, among the men especially. None got drunk, but some of them stayed pretty well keyed up.

On the morning following the third night of dancing we caught our horses and started back to camp, a tired bunch. When we got there it was not to bed and to sleep, but to work until dark. We had to ride the line and make up for the three days we were away. It was long after dark when we hit our wolf hides. We were a week getting over the effects of the dance, and I expect the women were longer than that. Before long, however, we were getting excited about the Dockum dance.

During the previous fall (1881), Mr. Dockum hauled lumber from Fort Worth and started building his storehouse, twenty by thirty feet. We prevailed on him to give us a Christmas tree and a dance. He agreed to do so, provided we would guarantee to buy all his Christmas goods, and not leave any on hand unsold. Several others and I made the guarantee. News of the dance spread counties around. When Christmas came, neither all the lumber for the house nor the Christmas goods had arrived on account of bad weather delaying the freighters. About the first week in March, Dockum sent us word that the lumber and goods had arrived. Several of us who had guaranteed to take the Christmas wares got together and set a date for the Christmas tree. We put it two weeks off so the news would have time to get around. The day before the occasion, several of us went to the brakes over by the Caprock and brought in a big cedar for the Christmas tree. We put it up in the store and spent next day decorating it.

About the same crowd came to it that afternoon that had been at Slaughter's dance. The tree was as big a success as if it had taken place on scheduled time. Everyone was in a festive mood. I suppose this was the first community Christmas tree ever held west of Fort Griffin. The next year the Matadors had a delayed tree. It also took place in March, because the things that had been ordered for it were nearly three months late getting in.

After the Christmas tree exercises were over, we started to dance. George Edwards did the fiddling again and Bill Petty the calling. This dance was a one-night affair, and nobody lost any time. While the boys were waiting turns in the sets, they hustled the coffee pot and smoked cigarettes, occasionally taking a Christmas "nip" from a bottle of Four Roses.

A few days before the dance John Garrison burned a large hole in one of his boots while trying to dry it over the camp fire. John was in a bad frame of mind while we were making preparations. I saw he was dying with envy, so I had him try on my boots. They fitted him to a quats' heel. I told him we would take it turn about; I would dance a set while he stayed outside the house, then I would go outside and let him wear my boots while he danced a set. We managed the thing so that no one suspected the exchange of footgear. That was one dance that my boots took part in nearly every set.

The dance broke up at sun-up, and we caught our horses and headed for our home ranges.

# CHAPTER XI

# EUVENCE GARCIA

CAPORAL IS THE TERM vaqueros use for the foreman of a roundup outfit. Euvence Garcia was one of the best caporals to ever ride for the world-famous King Ranch of South Texas.

Frank Goodwyn, author of *Life on the King Ranch,* from which the story of Euvence is taken, grew up among the vaqueros on the Norias division of this vast ranching empire. His experiences with and observations of Euvence and the vaqueros of "Cow Camp Number Two" symbolize the manner in which the Anglo cowboys originally learned their craft from the Mexican vaqueros. This is one of the very few books to offer any real information on Mexican vaqueros. They were, to use a phrase coined by Encino Press's Bill Wittliff, the "Genesis of the Texas cowboy."

There remains material for several good books in the South Texas *brasada* and the brushpoppers, both Mexican and Anglo, who work in that rough country which was the cradle of the entire range cattle industry. Goodwyn only scratched the surface of the wealth of cowboy history that is the heritage of the brush country that lies between the Nueces River and the Rio Grande.

From *Life on the King Ranch,* by Frank Goodwyn, published by Thomas Y. Crowell Company, 1951. Reprinted with permission of Harper and Row Publishers, Inc.

Euvence is representative of several generations of good vaqueros. The legacy of his breed was never stated better than in a conversation Bill Wittliff had with a vaquero while photographing on a ranch in northern Mexico:

"For how long, I wanted to know, had he been a vaquero. For a time of twenty years, he told me, from the age of six years.

" 'Your father also?' I asked.

" 'Si. Un vaquero.'

" 'And your grandfather?'

" 'Un vaquero.'

"There was a silence. 'Vaqueros siempre.' Vaqueros always, he said finally. 'Desde el comienzo.' Since the beginning."

---

THERE ARE THOSE who have been swallowed by the brush. It is a creeping, savage thing that will not leave you the same, once you have gone into it. The clusters of thorny, fantastically shaped shrubs, seldom over ten feet tall, threaten and tease your tender eyes till you see all things differently. You have to fight it all the time you are in it, and while fighting you lose your old self.

Euvence Garcia, foreman of Cow Camp Number Two, had fought the brush all his life. The signs and movements of a normal man were therefore gone from him. He was bent, bowlegged, apparently crippled, though he did not actually limp. He seemed barely able to move about, rubbing his belly, grunting and uttering long, agonized "ah's." When you saw him for the first time you wondered: How many more seconds will he last? How long will he stand swaying before he falls? How much of a soul is there left in that poor gnarled body?

But let him mount a horse and get a rope in his hand, and he was a different being altogether. The brush and the dust were his true element. He was no longer the pitifully inadequate old creature that hobbled about the camp but a champion to compare with the knights of King Arthur. The rope was like a live thing in his hands, striking always the moment when its victim was most susceptible.

Once Euvence was chasing two wild colts down a lane chopped through the brush. He was alone and his own horse happened to be swift but no good for holding roped animals, especially colts half his age. You need a tall fleet horse with a seasoned cow eye for running in the brush, but for roping you want a stocky, strong-limbed beast that can pull against your victim.

Euvence knew that he could never hold these colts if he tried to rope them in the ordinary way, so he took the rope off the horn of his saddle, roped one of the colts with the regular loop, then made a new loop in the other end of the rope. All this time, he was running full drive, and he had to hold his reins tight to keep his own horse from stumbling over stumps. He held his reins in his teeth while making the new loop, for he had to have both hands free.

With the new loop he roped the other colt. Now he had hold of the middle of the rope. There was a colt on each end and his own horse was puffing like a steam engine. The stumps of chopped trees, whizzing by, raised ominous scarred heads all around them. The rope was long and loose, dangling sometimes almost to the ground.

Taking up a little of the slack, Euvence flung it down over the next big stump that came into his view. The stump was stronger than colts and saddle horse combined. When the colts hit the end of the rope, they were jerked flat on their sides by the jolt and lay panting in the sand.

Euvence leaped from his saddle and pulled enough slack into the rope to put a half hitch on the stump. By the time the colts recovered from the shock of their fall they were tied to the stump like two gentle sheep.

Tales like these are told of Euvence all over the southern point of Texas. "There was never a man like Garcia," they say for miles around. He is even extolled by those who have never seen him but only aspire one day to become fine vaqueros themselves.

When I went to Cow Camp Number Two, Euvence became my second father. My own father spent some time in the camp but had to leave it often to attend to other things. Nobody would have ever known that Euvence was watching after my safety. He talked to me as if I were grown, and that made me feel good.

He liked to take cold baths every morning in the water troughs— without soap, of course, because soap would spoil the drinking water for the cattle. I also was addicted to cold baths, and we soon got to taking them together.

Long before the bell of the remuda mare began to twang, I would be awakened by his thick voice and see him sitting on his cot, rubbing his belly and saying, "Esta amaneciendo." ("It is coming morning.") Then I'd roll out and the two of us would go for a cold dip, and he would greet the stimulating tang of the water with loud "ah's" and with resounding slaps on his deformed-looking thighs.

Euvence had a leatherlike face kept firm by much activity. In the starlight, it sparkled with the cool water from the trough. Then when the remuda bell began to clank he would step out of the bath, shake himself like a half-drowned dog, and put on his clothes without drying off. He liked the feel of cold, soaked clothes against his skin: the sharp nip of evaporating moisture. Later in the day, he got the same feeling from sweat drawn out of hot pores by the sun.

I didn't like all this at first, but once accustomed to it I would feel my own body hungering when denied it. We seldom wore shirts or underclothes. Only khaki jackets on our bare skins, so the wind could get into the sleeves and around our backs and cool us.

I had headaches and dizzy spells at first from the sharp contrasts between cold sweat and blood heated by much movement. When I complained, old Euvence would say yes, he suffered from the same thing. I believed him then, though I later suspected that he was only trying to make me feel better by acting like a companion in discomfort. After a month or so I got used to life in Cow Camp Number Two and then the dizzy spells and headaches went away.

Euvence never noticed any of my weaknesses. He just ignored them. For he was a past master at handling people as well as cows and horses. I remember once Eugenio Cantu, a heavy-set young man with a small mustache, full of high spirits and energy, decided to render Euvence the respectful service that earlier foremen had always exacted as a matter of course. In other corridas the caporals, basking in their own importance, would sit by the fire drinking coffee and order one of the hands to rope and saddle their horses. Euvence never did this, but always plodded with his creeping old gait out into the remuda and caught his own horse.

This must not be, thought Eugenio. The caporal himself out there in the dust, hours before daylight, doing something that a mere menial could have done for him? Garcia was old, and his creaking bones were too dear to be misused in such a way. Eugenio decided to put a stop to it. He was young and unimportant. He would rope and saddle the caporal's horse. He would do it secretly, for a surprise.

The feat was not easy, for the old man got up early. One morning, however, Eugenio went to meet the remuda when Euvence and I were still bathing in the trough. He knew the caporal's horses well. In preparation for this big achievement, he had been studying them for days. This morning the caporal would want to ride a tall, trotting bay, for they would be making a roundup in the Plain of the Garden, a stretch of flat ground that bristled with small mesquites. A good brush horse would be needed.

Eugenio found the tall bay with no trouble, flung a loop on him, and led him to where the foreman's saddle was thrown over a long horizontal pole that extended between two forked trees. The squeak of rubbing leather that the saddle made when moved was bothersome to Eugenio. He feared it would attract the caporal's attention and spoil the surprise. As quickly as he could, he flung the saddle on the horse over the two thick pads that the caporal used. He girted it loose, for he knew Euvence liked it that way and tightened it only when roping.

When the job was done, Eugenio hurried back to the foreman's cot, where Euvence had just returned from his bath and was starting for his saddle to get his rope. Seeing this, Eugenio slunk to one side

*His years as a vaquero are gallantly displayed on his face* (The Dobie
Collection, University of Texas, Austin)

and let the old man pass by to be surprised at the sight of his horse already saddled.

"Ah! Who did this?" exclaimed the famous man.

The servant was not slow to show himself. "I, señor! I thought you would want the tall boy today, since the Plain of the Garden requires a good brush horse."

"Yes! You are right! The tall boy!" Euvence's thick voice was thickened more by his emotion. "He is exactly the one I was going to catch! Thank you. You are a good man, Eugenio."

All day, Eugenio told me afterwards, those words ran through his young, ambitious head, making him giddy in his happiness. "You are a good man, Eugenio." All the corrida would know soon. When the caporal said it, it was so.

Eugenio would keep on being a good man. He would rope and saddle the caporal's horse every morning from now on. He would study the caporal's string of ponies and know beforehand just which one he would need. The stout dun named Doscientos for tomorrow, when the roundup would be at Agua Gorda, a broad open plain in the salt air of the Gulf coast, where much roping was usually done. For day after tomorrow, when they would work in pens, a young paint named San Saba would be good; for the next day, the sorrel Fandango, and so on. Eugenio thrilled at such a future; such a prospect of expressing his adoration for his ideal.

He slept soundly that night, dreaming beautiful dreams of this new heavenly role that he had given himself. From one of the sweetest of those dreams he was awakened by a gentle tap on his shoulder. He rubbed and opened his sleepy eyes. The first thing he saw were the stars, and they reminded him of the goodness into which he had been lifted. Next he saw the trees around the cot, and their stillness told him that another wonderful dawn was on its way. Another dawn melodious with the memory of those words, "You are a good man, Eugenio."

Who had tapped his shoulder? Opening his eyes again, Eugenio saw that it was none other than Euvence, the caporal himself, rubbing and patting his old belly and saying, "Eugenio? Did you want the little black, baldfaced mare for today? I have put your saddle on her. She will serve you well at Agua Gorda."

After that, Eugenio kept his rope for his own horses, and his admiration for Euvence mellowed into lifelong love.

Euvence seldom fired a man, but when a vaquero became a drawback to the corrida, there were ways of encouraging him to have to leave. They tell of one fellow who came to work for Euvence but was so clumsy that he should have been discharged at once. Yet he had not the sense to see his own worthlessness. He was insulted when others tried to tell him what to do. He was a conceited fool, blind to his own blunders. All the men expected and hoped that the foreman would give him his accounts and show him the road to Norias, but this was not Euvence's way. He never once hinted that the fellow was no good.

But one morning in the remuda he called the clumsy vaquero over and said, "Senon, you see that little paint horse over there by the gray mare? I want you to ride him today. He needs a good man on him for the morning."

That paint was an old spoiled horse: a horse that did not like work and had learned how to get out of it by waiting till his rider was settled and suspected nothing. When the time was ripe he would plunge into a bucking orgy, twisting and squawling and leaping till he had shaken the cowboy loose.

Senon saddled him with no trouble at all, but when he was only a few miles from camp, the paint went into his routine. Senon landed in the sand, knocking down a score of weeds, dazed and wondering what had struck him. The rest of the morning he spent on foot, chasing after the paint, bedraggled and cursing. Finally, one of the other men roped the paint and returned him to his unwilling rider. Euvence sat on his horse by the herd, laughing to himself and pretending not to see any of this.

Some time later, he approached Senon. The fellow was remounted but still battered and morose.

"Well, Senon, how are things going with you today?"

"Badly."

"Badly? Why badly?"

"This horse."

"Yes? A good, strong, spirited horse, isn't he?"

"But he took me by surprise."

"Oh, well. That's because he is not yet fully acquainted with you. After a few months of riding him, he will come to know you better and you will come to know him better. Then you will be more accustomed to one another. Look out!"

The paint had taken advantage of the conversation to go into another one of his favorite performances. He pawed the moon. He became a big ball of swerving, squealing dynamite. Senon lost his stirrup. He hugged the saddle horn until it jabbed him in the stomach and with another plunge of the horse he went sprawling belly down, arms outspread like the wings of an eagle about to light. He landed at the feet of Euvence's horse with his pants almost pulled off because his belt had raked up a whole row of weeds by the roots.

Under the film of dust from the herd, Euvence laughed till he was blue in the face. Senon rolled over, the dust around his mouth turned to mud by a mixture of sweat, tears, and blood from his battered nose.

The caporal got down and helped the fellow up. The paint was already a hundred yards away, headed for the brush at a jaunty lope.

"Don't worry, Senon," said Euvence. "One of the boys will catch your horse and bring him back to you."

Next morning, the foreman again called Senon over and said, "Senon, I think today you would like to ride that tall roan mare. The one with the white front legs. She is swift in the brush, and we work in brushy land today."

Senon gratefully saddled the roan mare. She had a habit of getting up a swift momentum then stopping suddenly for no reason except to see if her rider wouldn't keep going through the air over her head. If he was good enough to cling to her through such a crisis, she would dart without warning under a low mesquite limb, in such a way as to make it brush the burden off. If this did not work, she had a bucking act of her own which was in every way as impressive and effective as the paint's.

With Senon she used all three of these devices, and they all worked, he being still a little stunned by his experience with the paint the day before. Unlike the paint, the roan mare did not run away after each triumph, but remained standing gently, with reins hanging loose, inviting the rider to try again.

That night at supper, Senon came to where the foreman was squatting under a tree with a plate of beans and rice. "Don Euvence," he said, "I have just heard that there is good work in the north, on the La Parra Ranch. They pay well and give Sunday off. I would like to go there and try it if I may."

"Well, Senon," replied the foreman, "I am glad to hear that the chances are good there. I don't know how well we will get along without you, but I think we can stumble on somehow. When you get to Norias, go to Uncle Mack at the hotel. Tell him you want to quit and he will give you your check. Would you like to ride one of your new horses to Norias?"

"No, señor. If I may I would rather have one of the old ones."

# CHAPTER XII

# CARL BENEDICT

BENEDICT'S BOOK, *A Tenderfoot Kid on Gyp Water,* is one of the titles of the "Range Life Series" referred to in connection with the Jim McCauley book in Chapter Four.

The "Tenderfoot Kid's" story deals with one season spent reping with the general roundup on the North Texas range in 1894. A "rep" represented his boss's brand on a general roundup, working right along with the rest of the outfit and cutting out and taking to home range any cattle gathered in his brand.

By the time of the roundup in this story, the open range was quickly disappearing. Fences and windmills were changing ranch life forever. Longhorn cattle were being bred out of existence by the English shorthorn breeds and trail driving had passed into history. Before long there would be nothing left of the rawhide times but the memories of the men who had been cowboys.

Benedict's reluctance to see the roundup come to an end symbolizes a greater meaning to the whole breed of Texas cowboys as the century drew to a close. The days when a man could roll his bed and drift wherever he pleased were about gone. "Progress" was fast coming to the cow country. Many a

From *A Tenderfoot Kid on Gyp Water,* by Carl Peters Benedict, published by the Texas Folklore Society, 1943.

Texas cowboy lived to see the day when they, like Carl Benedict, would hate to see the changes that had come to the country "where once we chased the big, free steers."

---

A FEW DAYS AFTER I RECOVERED the sorrel 7 D L pony, Ward Dwight and I cut our cattle out of the day herd and set out for Brazile's place. We got to a deserted pen, about half way, close to sundown, and had the worst time two men ever had trying to pen those cattle. There was nothing but a little cedar rail pen, big enough to hold maybe three hundred head. It was built on an open place, and had one short wing running out from the gate about thirty steps. This wing allowed the cattle to circle clear around the corral. We had about two hundred head, with five or six old wild cows and some two-year-old steers among them. We could run them up close together, and by riding hard we could drive them right up to the gate. One of the wild cows would always be in the lead; then, looking in the gate, she would give a loud sniff and tear out, taking most of the cattle with her. When this happened, and it happened six or seven times, one of us would have to stay and hold the cattle that did not run off, while the other brought back the ones that got away. Ward and I took it time about, bringing them back.

By dark we had most of them in the pen. Then a bob-tailed two-year-old steer stuck the stub of his tail straight up in the air and darted off, taking about twenty head with him. Yelling to Ward to watch the gate, I took down my rope and whipped that steer around the corral twice. I was riding the little sorrel Shiloh pony, the fastest in my mount, and when the bob-tailed steer dropped his stub of a tail and broke away through the mesquite, it did not take us long to catch him. Ward said that when he rode up, I was standing on the ground, trying to beat that bob-tail steer to death with my rope. He said he sure thought I was killed when he came to hunt me, as there were some awful holes around that pen, and it was getting too dark to see. Ward had shut the gate, nearly all the cattle being in the pen. Turning bob-tail loose, we drove him to the other cattle that had run off and put them all in a little horse trap, or pasture, near the house.

The cattle woke up several times that night, walking around the corral and hooking each other with their long horns. We made our bed down close to the corral gate, after staking the two night horses and hobbling the rest and eating a little snack. The cattle would have had to run over us to get out the gate. The morning star came up on time, and it did not take us long to broil some bacon and boil some coffee in an old tin can, to down with cold biscuits.

I rode the big bay Ida horse that morning. Ward offered to bet me a dollar that I could not spur him and get away with it, but we did not make the bet. He flinched and snorted a little when the saddle was eased upon his back, but I held him carefully while girting the saddle on good, patted him on the neck and led him off a few steps to open the gate so the cattle could come out. By the time they were all out of the pen and I had shut the gate, my horse had the kink out of his back and trotted off like an old cowhorse. No one ever called me a bronc rider. There are lots of things one can do, if he wants to, that will keep a horse from pitching. Like many of his kind, Ida was all right after you trotted him off fifty or sixty yards in the morning, but if he was dashed off suddenly, as quick as the rider mounted, he would "call" for his man, every time.

Soon after we left camp that morning, we got up in the cedar brake country, and the five or six old cows kept giving trouble for a couple of hours. They were not so wild as they were just mean and contrary. They always walked up in the lead, and when they reached a brushy place, they would slip into the cedars, and one of us would have to lope up to the front and turn them back. Sometimes one of us would ride in front for half a mile holding them back. When we dropped back to the rear of the herd to help drive the rest of the cattle, we had to keep a sharp eye to the front. However, the farther cattle are driven the better they behave. Our old cows were behaving well when we reached Brazile's that evening. Will Lanier had got well and he came over and helped us shape up my employer's cattle for delivery to the Childress buyers. We got together about 700 head

*Preparing chuck for the outfit* (author's collection)

of stock besides the calves, delivered them at around $10 for the cows, calves not counted, $11 per head for the two-year-old steers. The bob-tailed steer had stayed in the bunch and he was behaving himself when I saw him walk past the bosses counting the cattle out on horseback.

Soon after this, we got word that the 8 wagon was coming up through Crowell and Mr. Arnett was going to work through the Witherspoon range and gather the rest of the 8 cattle and get all that the rest of us had gathered that summer. Getting everything ready, Will Lanier and I again set out, with two mounts of horses and a bed roll. A remnant of cattle in our brands were still to be picked up. I knew this would be the last work of the year, as it was nearly October now and they did not work late in the fall in that part of the country.

We found the 8 wagon near Crowell, and all the boys that had been with them in the spring were still along. Cap Weatherly and his brother Harry, McGinty, Mr. Arnett, Cal Lowry, the cook, and the rest of us all had a big time telling jokes. Ward Dwight had come down to work with us through the river range, and he told the boys all about the trouble I had with the bob-tailed steer. I had grown to be very fond of these men. In the spring I had started out such a "tenderfoot" that I did not know how to tie up my bed roll; now I felt that I was making a pretty good hand. I knew that any of the men would have killed a good horse to help me in case of trouble. We worked for a couple of weeks through the flat country, and were just going up into the hills, when the blow fell that put an end to my good times. We had just made the "Copper Mine" roundup, so called because something called an old "mine" was near the roundup ground.

I was coming in from the herd with some of the other men to change horses, when Mr. Brazile's nephew, Tobe Brazile, rode out from the wagon and told me that his uncle had bought the remnant of cattle we were gathering and that my employer had sent word for me to come in and bring my horses to Mr. Brazile's place. Knowing that this was the last of those happy days, it was with a heavy heart that I caught a fresh horse and walked up to eat my last meal with the chuck wagon. I could not talk much and when the time came to say good bye, it was hard for me to look like a wild, bad cowpuncher.

Ward Dwight was the last man I spoke to. He shook hands when I told him good bye, we looked at each other, and I turned around and rode off feeling that all the joy had gone out of my life. As Ward had helped me cut my horses and drive them away from the remuda, it took but a few minutes for me to put them in a steady trot.

When I got about a half mile from the wagon, I turned once and looked for a long minute at the men working with the herd on the open prairie, at the wagon with the cook going around washing the dishes, and at the wrang taking his horses out to find the best spots of grass to graze them on. That night I rode into Mr. Brazile's place and the next morning started back to the "lower country," as they called the settlements.

For a long time I did not see any of the boys that worked up there. Some of them I have never seen. I have never been back to that country, and do not want to go back, because it would be painful to me to see the open prairies where we used to throw the roundups together, now cut up into farms, and to hear farmers' cow-bells jingling in the Pease River breaks where once we chased the big, free steers.

# EPILOGUE

THERE IS A WIDELY HELD NOTION that the Texas cowboy is an extinct species, that he belongs to history and has receded into the dim past along with longhorn cattle and open ranges. This perspective is supported by the weight of almost the entirety of cowboy bibliography. Cowboy books, like cowboy movies, concentrate on the historical figure of the cowboy and only rarely pay attention to contemporary cowpunchers.

I suspect that this inequity has something to do with the elements of drama and romance which were more apparent in the days when cowboys wore six-shooters and followed longhorns up the trails from Texas to places with exotic-sounding names like Ogallala and Cheyenne.

Whatever the reasons, the Texas cowpuncher of today has gone about his work unnoticed for the most part by those who believe his kind to have been an early victim of barbed wire and modern technology.

There is still more of them around than most people think. They share a pride in their work with those who rode before them. The same kind of reasons that made farm boys leave home to follow up the trails out of Texas still move boys to take after cowpunching. Although the range has been fenced and there are no longer trail drives of the size the West once knew, there is still plenty of the same kind of wild action that has always gone with men on horseback working around cattle.

The boys who work on Texas ranches today have to like their kind of life. Although wages have improved since the open range days, they still are not good enough to attract any kind of man to the task of carrying on the traditions of the cowboy. A man who makes his living today on somebody else's ranch as a working cowhand is attracted to the life by something more than the money.

A fierce sense of independence is an unmistakable trait in today's cowboy just as it was in the men of the rawhide times. There is a kind of satisfaction that comes with working around cattle. Most cowhands could not put a reason into words, but if you offered them the choice of living on the ranch, working on horseback all day, out in all kinds of weather, roping, doctoring and seeing after cattle and horses, or putting in eight hours in an air-conditioned office and living in a suburban housing tract, they would not have to think long before making their choice.

The work is not easy. Cutting and branding calves and colts in the choking dust of a working pen, breaking ice on troughs and water holes, sitting up all night with first-calf heifers, mending and building fence, feeding in the winter and drought times, pulling a water well, or repairing a windmill are but a few of the ordinary tasks that have to be done. But they get done. They get done by boys and men who could be making more money in another line of work with considerably less physical effort.

According to the modern prejudices of society, the men who stay in the saddle as working cowhands do so because of a lack of responsibility or initiative. The truth is that cowboys are not much inclined to philosophy. They do not spend much time wondering why they do what they do. They just know what it feels like to be horseback in a remote pasture where it seems just as it must have a hundred years ago. They know how they feel when they have roped and thrown a big steer with the help of a good horse. They like the feel of a new hat or pair of boots. They are the ones who can tell you what the world looks like at sunup any time of the year. They do not have to look at a calendar to tell when the seasons change, and a clock is not very important, either.

Cowboys will go on doing what they do as long as they can find their kind of work, and after that, they will talk about it and remember how it was. There will always be others to come along after them, too — boys proud to be Texans, who will strap on a pair of spurs and carry on the business of cowboying.

The cow country is not the same as it was when Teddy Blue and Charlie Siringo were riding. Pickup trucks, hydraulic cattle chutes, feed lots and many other innovations have changed the face and the nature of the range. The process of change continues today. Cowboys who were born too late to take part in the pageant of the open range have lived to see their own brand of cowboying change, too. There will be a time when men who ride around cattle today will remember the "old days" and lament their passing. As long as there are cattle there will be cowboys.

Because cattle are such that their welfare cannot be trusted to a machine, and because there will always be men who will want the chance to do a man's job ahorseback, there will still be booted and big-hatted men who are more comfortable in the saddle than on the ground. There will still be satisfaction in seeing a well-thrown loop settle around the base of a pair of moving horns and of staying with a horse that humps his back and goes to pitching on a frosty morning.

Cowboys and cattle are an indelible and vital part of what Texas was and is yet. The cattle business remains a significant factor in the economy of modern Texas. Sociologically, the figure of the cowboy constitutes a symbol which reflects the vitality of the people of the state. Historically, the story of the cowboy is the most basic fiber in the proud Texas heritage.

While the cowboy's golden age is now a part of Lone Star history, he is still a viable character, and Texas is his natural home. There will always be cowboys in the Lone Star State.